C-4116 CAREER EXAMINATION SERIES

This is your
PASSBOOK for...

Supervisor II (Social Work)

Test Preparation Study Guide
Questions & Answers

NATIONAL LEARNING CORPORATION®

COPYRIGHT NOTICE

This book is SOLELY intended for, is sold ONLY to, and its use is RESTRICTED to individual, bona fide applicants or candidates who qualify by virtue of having seriously filed applications for appropriate license, certificate, professional and/or promotional advancement, higher school matriculation, scholarship, or other legitimate requirements of education and/or governmental authorities.

This book is NOT intended for use, class instruction, tutoring, training, duplication, copying, reprinting, excerption, or adaptation, etc., by:

1) Other publishers
2) Proprietors and/or Instructors of "Coaching" and/or Preparatory Courses
3) Personnel and/or Training Divisions of commercial, industrial, and governmental organizations
4) Schools, colleges, or universities and/or their departments and staffs, including teachers and other personnel
5) Testing Agencies or Bureaus
6) Study groups which seek by the purchase of a single volume to copy and/or duplicate and/or adapt this material for use by the group as a whole without having purchased individual volumes for each of the members of the group
7) Et al.

Such persons would be in violation of appropriate Federal and State statutes.

PROVISION OF LICENSING AGREEMENTS – Recognized educational, commercial, industrial, and governmental institutions and organizations, and others legitimately engaged in educational pursuits, including training, testing, and measurement activities, may address request for a licensing agreement to the copyright owners, who will determine whether, and under what conditions, including fees and charges, the materials in this book may be used them. In other words, a licensing facility exists for the legitimate use of the material in this book on other than an individual basis. However, it is asseverated and affirmed here that the material in this book CANNOT be used without the receipt of the express permission of such a licensing agreement from the Publishers. Inquiries re licensing should be addressed to the company, attention rights and permissions department.

All rights reserved, including the right of reproduction in whole or in part, in any form or by any means, electronic or mechanical, including photocopying, recording, or by any information storage and retrieval system, without permission in writing from the Publisher.

Copyright © 2025 by
National Learning Corporation

212 Michael Drive, Syosset, NY 11791
(516) 921-8888 • www.passbooks.com
E-mail: info@passbooks.com

PASSBOOK® SERIES

THE *PASSBOOK® SERIES* has been created to prepare applicants and candidates for the ultimate academic battlefield – the examination room.

At some time in our lives, each and every one of us may be required to take an examination – for validation, matriculation, admission, qualification, registration, certification, or licensure.

Based on the assumption that every applicant or candidate has met the basic formal educational standards, has taken the required number of courses, and read the necessary texts, the *PASSBOOK® SERIES* furnishes the one special preparation which may assure passing with confidence, instead of failing with insecurity. Examination questions – together with answers – are furnished as the basic vehicle for study so that the mysteries of the examination and its compounding difficulties may be eliminated or diminished by a sure method.

This book is meant to help you pass your examination provided that you qualify and are serious in your objective.

The entire field is reviewed through the huge store of content information which is succinctly presented through a provocative and challenging approach – the question-and-answer method.

A climate of success is established by furnishing the correct answers at the end of each test.

You soon learn to recognize types of questions, forms of questions, and patterns of questioning. You may even begin to anticipate expected outcomes.

You perceive that many questions are repeated or adapted so that you can gain acute insights, which may enable you to score many sure points.

You learn how to confront new questions, or types of questions, and to attack them confidently and work out the correct answers.

You note objectives and emphases, and recognize pitfalls and dangers, so that you may make positive educational adjustments.

Moreover, you are kept fully informed in relation to new concepts, methods, practices, and directions in the field.

You discover that you are actually taking the examination all the time: you are preparing for the examination by "taking" an examination, not by reading extraneous and/or supererogatory textbooks.

In short, this PASSBOOK®, used directedly, should be an important factor in helping you to pass your test.

SUPERVISOR II (SOCIAL WORK)

DUTIES
Supervisors II (Social Work), under direction, supervise a number of social work units, providing psychosocial services in such settings as social service centers, public housing, prisons, health care facilities and shelters, to individual clients/patients, or to families and/or other groups of adults/children, utilizing casework, group work or community organization methodologies; or supervise groups of professional staff performing program evaluation and social work planning; and/or perform highly complex program evaluation and planning work for the agency. All Supervisors II (Social Work) perform related work.

SCOPE OF THE EXAMINATION
The written test will cover knowledge, skills and abilities in such areas as:

1. Case histories in social services casework programs;
2. Administrative supervision;
3. Preparing written material; and
4. Organization and administration of social services casework programs.

HOW TO TAKE A TEST

I. YOU MUST PASS AN EXAMINATION

A. *WHAT EVERY CANDIDATE SHOULD KNOW*

Examination applicants often ask us for help in preparing for the written test. What can I study in advance? What kinds of questions will be asked? How will the test be given? How will the papers be graded?

As an applicant for a civil service examination, you may be wondering about some of these things. Our purpose here is to suggest effective methods of advance study and to describe civil service examinations.

Your chances for success on this examination can be increased if you know how to prepare. Those "pre-examination jitters" can be reduced if you know what to expect. You can even experience an adventure in good citizenship if you know why civil service exams are given.

B. *WHY ARE CIVIL SERVICE EXAMINATIONS GIVEN?*

Civil service examinations are important to you in two ways. As a citizen, you want public jobs filled by employees who know how to do their work. As a job seeker, you want a fair chance to compete for that job on an equal footing with other candidates. The best-known means of accomplishing this two-fold goal is the competitive examination.

Exams are widely publicized throughout the nation. They may be administered for jobs in federal, state, city, municipal, town or village governments or agencies.

Any citizen may apply, with some limitations, such as the age or residence of applicants. Your experience and education may be reviewed to see whether you meet the requirements for the particular examination. When these requirements exist, they are reasonable and applied consistently to all applicants. Thus, a competitive examination may cause you some uneasiness now, but it is your privilege and safeguard.

C. *HOW ARE CIVIL SERVICE EXAMS DEVELOPED?*

Examinations are carefully written by trained technicians who are specialists in the field known as "psychological measurement," in consultation with recognized authorities in the field of work that the test will cover. These experts recommend the subject matter areas or skills to be tested; only those knowledges or skills important to your success on the job are included. The most reliable books and source materials available are used as references. Together, the experts and technicians judge the difficulty level of the questions.

Test technicians know how to phrase questions so that the problem is clearly stated. Their ethics do not permit "trick" or "catch" questions. Questions may have been tried out on sample groups, or subjected to statistical analysis, to determine their usefulness.

Written tests are often used in combination with performance tests, ratings of training and experience, and oral interviews. All of these measures combine to form the best-known means of finding the right person for the right job.

II. HOW TO PASS THE WRITTEN TEST

A. NATURE OF THE EXAMINATION

To prepare intelligently for civil service examinations, you should know how they differ from school examinations you have taken. In school you were assigned certain definite pages to read or subjects to cover. The examination questions were quite detailed and usually emphasized memory. Civil service exams, on the other hand, try to discover your present ability to perform the duties of a position, plus your potentiality to learn these duties. In other words, a civil service exam attempts to predict how successful you will be. Questions cover such a broad area that they cannot be as minute and detailed as school exam questions.

In the public service similar kinds of work, or positions, are grouped together in one "class." This process is known as *position-classification*. All the positions in a class are paid according to the salary range for that class. One class title covers all of these positions, and they are all tested by the same examination.

B. FOUR BASIC STEPS

1) Study the announcement

How, then, can you know what subjects to study? Our best answer is: "Learn as much as possible about the class of positions for which you've applied." The exam will test the knowledge, skills and abilities needed to do the work.

Your most valuable source of information about the position you want is the official exam announcement. This announcement lists the training and experience qualifications. Check these standards and apply only if you come reasonably close to meeting them.

The brief description of the position in the examination announcement offers some clues to the subjects which will be tested. Think about the job itself. Review the duties in your mind. Can you perform them, or are there some in which you are rusty? Fill in the blank spots in your preparation.

Many jurisdictions preview the written test in the exam announcement by including a section called "Knowledge and Abilities Required," "Scope of the Examination," or some similar heading. Here you will find out specifically what fields will be tested.

2) Review your own background

Once you learn in general what the position is all about, and what you need to know to do the work, ask yourself which subjects you already know fairly well and which need improvement. You may wonder whether to concentrate on improving your strong areas or on building some background in your fields of weakness. When the announcement has specified "some knowledge" or "considerable knowledge," or has used adjectives like "beginning principles of..." or "advanced ... methods," you can get a clue as to the number and difficulty of questions to be asked in any given field. More questions, and hence broader coverage, would be included for those subjects which are more important in the work. Now weigh your strengths and weaknesses against the job requirements and prepare accordingly.

3) Determine the level of the position

Another way to tell how intensively you should prepare is to understand the level of the job for which you are applying. Is it the entering level? In other words, is this the position in which beginners in a field of work are hired? Or is it an intermediate or advanced level? Sometimes this is indicated by such words as "Junior" or "Senior" in the class title. Other jurisdictions use Roman numerals to designate the level – Clerk I, Clerk II, for example. The word "Supervisor" sometimes appears in the title. If the level is not indicated by the title, check the description of duties. Will you be working under very close supervision, or will you have responsibility for independent decisions in this work?

4) Choose appropriate study materials

Now that you know the subjects to be examined and the relative amount of each subject to be covered, you can choose suitable study materials. For beginning level jobs, or even advanced ones, if you have a pronounced weakness in some aspect of your training, read a modern, standard textbook in that field. Be sure it is up to date and has general coverage. Such books are normally available at your library, and the librarian will be glad to help you locate one. For entry-level positions, questions of appropriate difficulty are chosen – neither highly advanced questions, nor those too simple. Such questions require careful thought but not advanced training.

If the position for which you are applying is technical or advanced, you will read more advanced, specialized material. If you are already familiar with the basic principles of your field, elementary textbooks would waste your time. Concentrate on advanced textbooks and technical periodicals. Think through the concepts and review difficult problems in your field.

These are all general sources. You can get more ideas on your own initiative, following these leads. For example, training manuals and publications of the government agency which employs workers in your field can be useful, particularly for technical and professional positions. A letter or visit to the government department involved may result in more specific study suggestions, and certainly will provide you with a more definite idea of the exact nature of the position you are seeking.

III. KINDS OF TESTS

Tests are used for purposes other than measuring knowledge and ability to perform specified duties. For some positions, it is equally important to test ability to make adjustments to new situations or to profit from training. In others, basic mental abilities not dependent on information are essential. Questions which test these things may not appear as pertinent to the duties of the position as those which test for knowledge and information. Yet they are often highly important parts of a fair examination. For very general questions, it is almost impossible to help you direct your study efforts. What we can do is to point out some of the more common of these general abilities needed in public service positions and describe some typical questions.

1) General information

Broad, general information has been found useful for predicting job success in some kinds of work. This is tested in a variety of ways, from vocabulary lists to questions about current events. Basic background in some field of work, such as sociology or economics, may be sampled in a group of questions. Often these are principles which have become familiar to most persons through exposure rather than through formal training. It is difficult to advise you how to study for these questions; being alert to the world around you is our best suggestion.

2) Verbal ability

An example of an ability needed in many positions is verbal or language ability. Verbal ability is, in brief, the ability to use and understand words. Vocabulary and grammar tests are typical measures of this ability. Reading comprehension or paragraph interpretation questions are common in many kinds of civil service tests. You are given a paragraph of written material and asked to find its central meaning.

3) Numerical ability

Number skills can be tested by the familiar arithmetic problem, by checking paired lists of numbers to see which are alike and which are different, or by interpreting charts and graphs. In the latter test, a graph may be printed in the test booklet which you are asked to use as the basis for answering questions.

4) Observation

A popular test for law-enforcement positions is the observation test. A picture is shown to you for several minutes, then taken away. Questions about the picture test your ability to observe both details and larger elements.

5) Following directions

In many positions in the public service, the employee must be able to carry out written instructions dependably and accurately. You may be given a chart with several columns, each column listing a variety of information. The questions require you to carry out directions involving the information given in the chart.

6) Skills and aptitudes

Performance tests effectively measure some manual skills and aptitudes. When the skill is one in which you are trained, such as typing or shorthand, you can practice. These tests are often very much like those given in business school or high school courses. For many of the other skills and aptitudes, however, no short-time preparation can be made. Skills and abilities natural to you or that you have developed throughout your lifetime are being tested.

Many of the general questions just described provide all the data needed to answer the questions and ask you to use your reasoning ability to find the answers. Your best preparation for these tests, as well as for tests of facts and ideas, is to be at your physical and mental best. You, no doubt, have your own methods of getting into an exam-taking mood and keeping "in shape." The next section lists some ideas on this subject.

IV. KINDS OF QUESTIONS

Only rarely is the "essay" question, which you answer in narrative form, used in civil service tests. Civil service tests are usually of the short-answer type. Full instructions for answering these questions will be given to you at the examination. But in case this is your first experience with short-answer questions and separate answer sheets, here is what you need to know:

1) Multiple-choice Questions

Most popular of the short-answer questions is the "multiple choice" or "best answer" question. It can be used, for example, to test for factual knowledge, ability to solve problems or judgment in meeting situations found at work.

A multiple-choice question is normally one of three types—
- It can begin with an incomplete statement followed by several possible endings. You are to find the one ending which *best* completes the statement, although some of the others may not be entirely wrong.
- It can also be a complete statement in the form of a question which is answered by choosing one of the statements listed.

- It can be in the form of a problem – again you select the best answer.

Here is an example of a multiple-choice question with a discussion which should give you some clues as to the method for choosing the right answer:

When an employee has a complaint about his assignment, the action which will *best* help him overcome his difficulty is to
    A. discuss his difficulty with his coworkers
    B. take the problem to the head of the organization
    C. take the problem to the person who gave him the assignment
    D. say nothing to anyone about his complaint

In answering this question, you should study each of the choices to find which is best. Consider choice "A" – Certainly an employee may discuss his complaint with fellow employees, but no change or improvement can result, and the complaint remains unresolved. Choice "B" is a poor choice since the head of the organization probably does not know what assignment you have been given, and taking your problem to him is known as "going over the head" of the supervisor. The supervisor, or person who made the assignment, is the person who can clarify it or correct any injustice. Choice "C" is, therefore, correct. To say nothing, as in choice "D," is unwise. Supervisors have and interest in knowing the problems employees are facing, and the employee is seeking a solution to his problem.

2) True/False Questions

The "true/false" or "right/wrong" form of question is sometimes used. Here a complete statement is given. Your job is to decide whether the statement is right or wrong.

SAMPLE: A roaming cell-phone call to a nearby city costs less than a non-roaming call to a distant city.

This statement is wrong, or false, since roaming calls are more expensive.
This is not a complete list of all possible question forms, although most of the others are variations of these common types. You will always get complete directions for answering questions. Be sure you understand *how* to mark your answers – ask questions until you do.

V. RECORDING YOUR ANSWERS

Computer terminals are used more and more today for many different kinds of exams.
For an examination with very few applicants, you may be told to record your answers in the test booklet itself. Separate answer sheets are much more common. If this separate answer sheet is to be scored by machine – and this is often the case – it is highly important that you mark your answers correctly in order to get credit.
An electronic scoring machine is often used in civil service offices because of the speed with which papers can be scored. Machine-scored answer sheets must be marked with a pencil, which will be given to you. This pencil has a high graphite content which responds to the electronic scoring machine. As a matter of fact, stray dots may register as answers, so do not let your pencil rest on the answer sheet while you are pondering the correct answer. Also, if your pencil lead breaks or is otherwise defective, ask for another.

Since the answer sheet will be dropped in a slot in the scoring machine, be careful not to bend the corners or get the paper crumpled.

The answer sheet normally has five vertical columns of numbers, with 30 numbers to a column. These numbers correspond to the question numbers in your test booklet. After each number, going across the page are four or five pairs of dotted lines. These short dotted lines have small letters or numbers above them. The first two pairs may also have a "T" or "F" above the letters. This indicates that the first two pairs only are to be used if the questions are of the true-false type. If the questions are multiple choice, disregard the "T" and "F" and pay attention only to the small letters or numbers.

Answer your questions in the manner of the sample that follows:

32. The largest city in the United States is
    A. Washington, D.C.
    B. New York City
    C. Chicago
    D. Detroit
    E. San Francisco

1) Choose the answer you think is best. (New York City is the largest, so "B" is correct.)
2) Find the row of dotted lines numbered the same as the question you are answering. (Find row number 32)
3) Find the pair of dotted lines corresponding to the answer. (Find the pair of lines under the mark "B.")
4) Make a solid black mark between the dotted lines.

VI. BEFORE THE TEST

Common sense will help you find procedures to follow to get ready for an examination. Too many of us, however, overlook these sensible measures. Indeed, nervousness and fatigue have been found to be the most serious reasons why applicants fail to do their best on civil service tests. Here is a list of reminders:

- Begin your preparation early – Don't wait until the last minute to go scurrying around for books and materials or to find out what the position is all about.
- Prepare continuously – An hour a night for a week is better than an all-night cram session. This has been definitely established. What is more, a night a week for a month will return better dividends than crowding your study into a shorter period of time.
- Locate the place of the exam – You have been sent a notice telling you when and where to report for the examination. If the location is in a different town or otherwise unfamiliar to you, it would be well to inquire the best route and learn something about the building.
- Relax the night before the test – Allow your mind to rest. Do not study at all that night. Plan some mild recreation or diversion; then go to bed early and get a good night's sleep.
- Get up early enough to make a leisurely trip to the place for the test – This way unforeseen events, traffic snarls, unfamiliar buildings, etc. will not upset you.
- Dress comfortably – A written test is not a fashion show. You will be known by number and not by name, so wear something comfortable.

- Leave excess paraphernalia at home – Shopping bags and odd bundles will get in your way. You need bring only the items mentioned in the official notice you received; usually everything you need is provided. Do not bring reference books to the exam. They will only confuse those last minutes and be taken away from you when in the test room.
- Arrive somewhat ahead of time – If because of transportation schedules you must get there very early, bring a newspaper or magazine to take your mind off yourself while waiting.
- Locate the examination room – When you have found the proper room, you will be directed to the seat or part of the room where you will sit. Sometimes you are given a sheet of instructions to read while you are waiting. Do not fill out any forms until you are told to do so; just read them and be prepared.
- Relax and prepare to listen to the instructions
- If you have any physical problem that may keep you from doing your best, be sure to tell the test administrator. If you are sick or in poor health, you really cannot do your best on the exam. You can come back and take the test some other time.

VII. AT THE TEST

The day of the test is here and you have the test booklet in your hand. The temptation to get going is very strong. Caution! There is more to success than knowing the right answers. You must know how to identify your papers and understand variations in the type of short-answer question used in this particular examination. Follow these suggestions for maximum results from your efforts:

1) Cooperate with the monitor

The test administrator has a duty to create a situation in which you can be as much at ease as possible. He will give instructions, tell you when to begin, check to see that you are marking your answer sheet correctly, and so on. He is not there to guard you, although he will see that your competitors do not take unfair advantage. He wants to help you do your best.

2) Listen to all instructions

Don't jump the gun! Wait until you understand all directions. In most civil service tests you get more time than you need to answer the questions. So don't be in a hurry. Read each word of instructions until you clearly understand the meaning. Study the examples, listen to all announcements and follow directions. Ask questions if you do not understand what to do.

3) Identify your papers

Civil service exams are usually identified by number only. You will be assigned a number; you must not put your name on your test papers. Be sure to copy your number correctly. Since more than one exam may be given, copy your exact examination title.

4) Plan your time

Unless you are told that a test is a "speed" or "rate of work" test, speed itself is usually not important. Time enough to answer all the questions will be provided, but this does not mean that you have all day. An overall time limit has been set. Divide the total time (in minutes) by the number of questions to determine the approximate time you have for each question.

5) Do not linger over difficult questions

If you come across a difficult question, mark it with a paper clip (useful to have along) and come back to it when you have been through the booklet. One caution if you do this – be sure to skip a number on your answer sheet as well. Check often to be sure that you have not lost your place and that you are marking in the row numbered the same as the question you are answering.

6) Read the questions

Be sure you know what the question asks! Many capable people are unsuccessful because they failed to *read* the questions correctly.

7) Answer all questions

Unless you have been instructed that a penalty will be deducted for incorrect answers, it is better to guess than to omit a question.

8) Speed tests

It is often better NOT to guess on speed tests. It has been found that on timed tests people are tempted to spend the last few seconds before time is called in marking answers at random – without even reading them – in the hope of picking up a few extra points. To discourage this practice, the instructions may warn you that your score will be "corrected" for guessing. That is, a penalty will be applied. The incorrect answers will be deducted from the correct ones, or some other penalty formula will be used.

9) Review your answers

If you finish before time is called, go back to the questions you guessed or omitted to give them further thought. Review other answers if you have time.

10) Return your test materials

If you are ready to leave before others have finished or time is called, take ALL your materials to the monitor and leave quietly. Never take any test material with you. The monitor can discover whose papers are not complete, and taking a test booklet may be grounds for disqualification.

VIII. EXAMINATION TECHNIQUES

1) Read the general instructions carefully. These are usually printed on the first page of the exam booklet. As a rule, these instructions refer to the timing of the examination; the fact that you should not start work until the signal and must stop work at a signal, etc. If there are any *special* instructions, such as a choice of questions to be answered, make sure that you note this instruction carefully.

2) When you are ready to start work on the examination, that is as soon as the signal has been given, read the instructions to each question booklet, underline any key words or phrases, such as *least, best, outline, describe* and the like. In this way you will tend to answer as requested rather than discover on reviewing your paper that you *listed without describing*, that you selected the *worst* choice rather than the *best* choice, etc.

3) If the examination is of the objective or multiple-choice type – that is, each question will also give a series of possible answers: A, B, C or D, and you are called upon to select the best answer and write the letter next to that answer on your answer paper – it is advisable to start answering each question in turn. There may be anywhere from 50 to 100 such questions in the three or four hours allotted and you can see how much time would be taken if you read through all the questions before beginning to answer any. Furthermore, if you come across a question or group of questions which you know would be difficult to answer, it would undoubtedly affect your handling of all the other questions.

4) If the examination is of the essay type and contains but a few questions, it is a moot point as to whether you should read all the questions before starting to answer any one. Of course, if you are given a choice – say five out of seven and the like – then it is essential to read all the questions so you can eliminate the two that are most difficult. If, however, you are asked to answer all the questions, there may be danger in trying to answer the easiest one first because you may find that you will spend too much time on it. The best technique is to answer the first question, then proceed to the second, etc.

5) Time your answers. Before the exam begins, write down the time it started, then add the time allowed for the examination and write down the time it must be completed, then divide the time available somewhat as follows:
    - If 3-1/2 hours are allowed, that would be 210 minutes. If you have 80 objective-type questions, that would be an average of 2-1/2 minutes per question. Allow yourself no more than 2 minutes per question, or a total of 160 minutes, which will permit about 50 minutes to review.
    - If for the time allotment of 210 minutes there are 7 essay questions to answer, that would average about 30 minutes a question. Give yourself only 25 minutes per question so that you have about 35 minutes to review.

6) The most important instruction is to *read each question* and make sure you know what is wanted. The second most important instruction is to *time yourself properly* so that you answer every question. The third most important instruction is to *answer every question*. Guess if you have to but include something for each question. Remember that you will receive no credit for a blank and will probably receive some credit if you write something in answer to an essay question. If you guess a letter – say "B" for a multiple-choice question – you may have guessed right. If you leave a blank as an answer to a multiple-choice question, the examiners may respect your feelings but it will not add a point to your score. Some exams may penalize you for wrong answers, so in such cases *only*, you may not want to guess unless you have some basis for your answer.

7) Suggestions
    a. Objective-type questions
        1. Examine the question booklet for proper sequence of pages and questions
        2. Read all instructions carefully
        3. Skip any question which seems too difficult; return to it after all other questions have been answered
        4. Apportion your time properly; do not spend too much time on any single question or group of questions

5. Note and underline key words – *all, most, fewest, least, best, worst, same, opposite*, etc.
6. Pay particular attention to negatives
7. Note unusual option, e.g., unduly long, short, complex, different or similar in content to the body of the question
8. Observe the use of "hedging" words – *probably, may, most likely*, etc.
9. Make sure that your answer is put next to the same number as the question
10. Do not second-guess unless you have good reason to believe the second answer is definitely more correct
11. Cross out original answer if you decide another answer is more accurate; do not erase until you are ready to hand your paper in
12. Answer all questions; guess unless instructed otherwise
13. Leave time for review

b. Essay questions
 1. Read each question carefully
 2. Determine exactly what is wanted. Underline key words or phrases.
 3. Decide on outline or paragraph answer
 4. Include many different points and elements unless asked to develop any one or two points or elements
 5. Show impartiality by giving pros and cons unless directed to select one side only
 6. Make and write down any assumptions you find necessary to answer the questions
 7. Watch your English, grammar, punctuation and choice of words
 8. Time your answers; don't crowd material

8) Answering the essay question

Most essay questions can be answered by framing the specific response around several key words or ideas. Here are a few such key words or ideas:

M's: manpower, materials, methods, money, management
P's: purpose, program, policy, plan, procedure, practice, problems, pitfalls, personnel, public relations

  a. Six basic steps in handling problems:
   1. Preliminary plan and background development
   2. Collect information, data and facts
   3. Analyze and interpret information, data and facts
   4. Analyze and develop solutions as well as make recommendations
   5. Prepare report and sell recommendations
   6. Install recommendations and follow up effectiveness

  b. Pitfalls to avoid
   1. *Taking things for granted* – A statement of the situation does not necessarily imply that each of the elements is necessarily true; for example, a complaint may be invalid and biased so that all that can be taken for granted is that a complaint has been registered

2. *Considering only one side of a situation* – Wherever possible, indicate several alternatives and then point out the reasons you selected the best one
3. *Failing to indicate follow up* – Whenever your answer indicates action on your part, make certain that you will take proper follow-up action to see how successful your recommendations, procedures or actions turn out to be
4. *Taking too long in answering any single question* – Remember to time your answers properly

IX. AFTER THE TEST

Scoring procedures differ in detail among civil service jurisdictions although the general principles are the same. Whether the papers are hand-scored or graded by machine we have described, they are nearly always graded by number. That is, the person who marks the paper knows only the number – never the name – of the applicant. Not until all the papers have been graded will they be matched with names. If other tests, such as training and experience or oral interview ratings have been given, scores will be combined. Different parts of the examination usually have different weights. For example, the written test might count 60 percent of the final grade, and a rating of training and experience 40 percent. In many jurisdictions, veterans will have a certain number of points added to their grades.

After the final grade has been determined, the names are placed in grade order and an eligible list is established. There are various methods for resolving ties between those who get the same final grade – probably the most common is to place first the name of the person whose application was received first. Job offers are made from the eligible list in the order the names appear on it. You will be notified of your grade and your rank as soon as all these computations have been made. This will be done as rapidly as possible.

People who are found to meet the requirements in the announcement are called "eligibles." Their names are put on a list of eligible candidates. An eligible's chances of getting a job depend on how high he stands on this list and how fast agencies are filling jobs from the list.

When a job is to be filled from a list of eligibles, the agency asks for the names of people on the list of eligibles for that job. When the civil service commission receives this request, it sends to the agency the names of the three people highest on this list. Or, if the job to be filled has specialized requirements, the office sends the agency the names of the top three persons who meet these requirements from the general list.

The appointing officer makes a choice from among the three people whose names were sent to him. If the selected person accepts the appointment, the names of the others are put back on the list to be considered for future openings.

That is the rule in hiring from all kinds of eligible lists, whether they are for typist, carpenter, chemist, or something else. For every vacancy, the appointing officer has his choice of any one of the top three eligibles on the list. This explains why the person whose name is on top of the list sometimes does not get an appointment when some of the persons lower on the list do. If the appointing officer chooses the second or third eligible, the No. 1 eligible does not get a job at once, but stays on the list until he is appointed or the list is terminated.

X. HOW TO PASS THE INTERVIEW TEST

The examination for which you applied requires an oral interview test. You have already taken the written test and you are now being called for the interview test – the final part of the formal examination.

You may think that it is not possible to prepare for an interview test and that there are no procedures to follow during an interview. Our purpose is to point out some things you can do in advance that will help you and some good rules to follow and pitfalls to avoid while you are being interviewed.

What is an interview supposed to test?

The written examination is designed to test the technical knowledge and competence of the candidate; the oral is designed to evaluate intangible qualities, not readily measured otherwise, and to establish a list showing the relative fitness of each candidate – as measured against his competitors – for the position sought. Scoring is not on the basis of "right" and "wrong," but on a sliding scale of values ranging from "not passable" to "outstanding." As a matter of fact, it is possible to achieve a relatively low score without a single "incorrect" answer because of evident weakness in the qualities being measured.

Occasionally, an examination may consist entirely of an oral test – either an individual or a group oral. In such cases, information is sought concerning the technical knowledges and abilities of the candidate, since there has been no written examination for this purpose. More commonly, however, an oral test is used to supplement a written examination.

Who conducts interviews?

The composition of oral boards varies among different jurisdictions. In nearly all, a representative of the personnel department serves as chairman. One of the members of the board may be a representative of the department in which the candidate would work. In some cases, "outside experts" are used, and, frequently, a businessman or some other representative of the general public is asked to serve. Labor and management or other special groups may be represented. The aim is to secure the services of experts in the appropriate field.

However the board is composed, it is a good idea (and not at all improper or unethical) to ascertain in advance of the interview who the members are and what groups they represent. When you are introduced to them, you will have some idea of their backgrounds and interests, and at least you will not stutter and stammer over their names.

What should be done before the interview?

While knowledge about the board members is useful and takes some of the surprise element out of the interview, there is other preparation which is more substantive. It *is* possible to prepare for an oral interview – in several ways:

1) Keep a copy of your application and review it carefully before the interview

This may be the only document before the oral board, and the starting point of the interview. Know what education and experience you have listed there, and the sequence and dates of all of it. Sometimes the board will ask you to review the highlights of your experience for them; you should not have to hem and haw doing it.

2) Study the class specification and the examination announcement

Usually, the oral board has one or both of these to guide them. The qualities, characteristics or knowledges required by the position sought are stated in these documents. They offer valuable clues as to the nature of the oral interview. For example, if the job involves supervisory responsibilities, the announcement will usually indicate that knowledge of modern supervisory methods and the qualifications of the candidate as a supervisor will be tested. If so, you can expect such questions, frequently in the form of a hypothetical situation which you are expected to solve. NEVER go into an oral without knowledge of the duties and responsibilities of the job you seek.

3) Think through each qualification required

Try to visualize the kind of questions you would ask if you were a board member. How well could you answer them? Try especially to appraise your own knowledge and background in each area, *measured against the job sought*, and identify any areas in which you are weak. Be critical and realistic – do not flatter yourself.

4) Do some general reading in areas in which you feel you may be weak

For example, if the job involves supervision and your past experience has NOT, some general reading in supervisory methods and practices, particularly in the field of human relations, might be useful. Do NOT study agency procedures or detailed manuals. The oral board will be testing your understanding and capacity, not your memory.

5) Get a good night's sleep and watch your general health and mental attitude

You will want a clear head at the interview. Take care of a cold or any other minor ailment, and of course, no hangovers.

What should be done on the day of the interview?

Now comes the day of the interview itself. Give yourself plenty of time to get there. Plan to arrive somewhat ahead of the scheduled time, particularly if your appointment is in the fore part of the day. If a previous candidate fails to appear, the board might be ready for you a bit early. By early afternoon an oral board is almost invariably behind schedule if there are many candidates, and you may have to wait. Take along a book or magazine to read, or your application to review, but leave any extraneous material in the waiting room when you go in for your interview. In any event, relax and compose yourself.

The matter of dress is important. The board is forming impressions about you – from your experience, your manners, your attitude, and your appearance. Give your personal appearance careful attention. Dress your best, but not your flashiest. Choose conservative, appropriate clothing, and be sure it is immaculate. This is a business interview, and your appearance should indicate that you regard it as such. Besides, being well groomed and properly dressed will help boost your confidence.

Sooner or later, someone will call your name and escort you into the interview room. *This is it.* From here on you are on your own. It is too late for any more preparation. But remember, you asked for this opportunity to prove your fitness, and you are here because your request was granted.

What happens when you go in?

The usual sequence of events will be as follows: The clerk (who is often the board stenographer) will introduce you to the chairman of the oral board, who will introduce you to the other members of the board. Acknowledge the introductions before you sit down. Do not be surprised if you find a microphone facing you or a stenotypist sitting by. Oral interviews are usually recorded in the event of an appeal or other review.

Usually the chairman of the board will open the interview by reviewing the highlights of your education and work experience from your application – primarily for the benefit of the other members of the board, as well as to get the material into the record. Do not interrupt or comment unless there is an error or significant misinterpretation; if that is the case, do not hesitate. But do not quibble about insignificant matters. Also, he will usually ask you some question about your education, experience or your present job – partly to get you to start talking and to establish the interviewing "rapport." He may start the actual questioning, or turn it over to one of the other members. Frequently, each member undertakes the questioning on a particular area, one in which he is perhaps most competent, so you can expect each member to participate in the examination. Because time is limited, you may also expect some rather abrupt switches in the direction the questioning takes, so do not be upset by it. Normally, a board member will not pursue a single line of questioning unless he discovers a particular strength or weakness.

After each member has participated, the chairman will usually ask whether any member has any further questions, then will ask you if you have anything you wish to add. Unless you are expecting this question, it may floor you. Worse, it may start you off on an extended, extemporaneous speech. The board is not usually seeking more information. The question is principally to offer you a last opportunity to present further qualifications or to indicate that you have nothing to add. So, if you feel that a significant qualification or characteristic has been overlooked, it is proper to point it out in a sentence or so. Do not compliment the board on the thoroughness of their examination – they have been sketchy, and you know it. If you wish, merely say, "No thank you, I have nothing further to add." This is a point where you can "talk yourself out" of a good impression or fail to present an important bit of information. Remember, *you close the interview yourself*.

The chairman will then say, "That is all, Mr. _____, thank you." Do not be startled; the interview is over, and quicker than you think. Thank him, gather your belongings and take your leave. Save your sigh of relief for the other side of the door.

How to put your best foot forward

Throughout this entire process, you may feel that the board individually and collectively is trying to pierce your defenses, seek out your hidden weaknesses and embarrass and confuse you. Actually, this is not true. They are obliged to make an appraisal of your qualifications for the job you are seeking, and they want to see you in your best light. Remember, they must interview all candidates and a non-cooperative candidate may become a failure in spite of their best efforts to bring out his qualifications. Here are 15 suggestions that will help you:

1) Be natural – Keep your attitude confident, not cocky

If you are not confident that you can do the job, do not expect the board to be. Do not apologize for your weaknesses, try to bring out your strong points. The board is interested in a positive, not negative, presentation. Cockiness will antagonize any board member and make him wonder if you are covering up a weakness by a false show of strength.

2) Get comfortable, but don't lounge or sprawl

Sit erectly but not stiffly. A careless posture may lead the board to conclude that you are careless in other things, or at least that you are not impressed by the importance of the occasion. Either conclusion is natural, even if incorrect. Do not fuss with your clothing, a pencil or an ashtray. Your hands may occasionally be useful to emphasize a point; do not let them become a point of distraction.

3) Do not wisecrack or make small talk

This is a serious situation, and your attitude should show that you consider it as such. Further, the time of the board is limited – they do not want to waste it, and neither should you.

4) Do not exaggerate your experience or abilities

In the first place, from information in the application or other interviews and sources, the board may know more about you than you think. Secondly, you probably will not get away with it. An experienced board is rather adept at spotting such a situation, so do not take the chance.

5) If you know a board member, do not make a point of it, yet do not hide it

Certainly you are not fooling him, and probably not the other members of the board. Do not try to take advantage of your acquaintanceship – it will probably do you little good.

6) Do not dominate the interview

Let the board do that. They will give you the clues – do not assume that you have to do all the talking. Realize that the board has a number of questions to ask you, and do not try to take up all the interview time by showing off your extensive knowledge of the answer to the first one.

7) Be attentive

You only have 20 minutes or so, and you should keep your attention at its sharpest throughout. When a member is addressing a problem or question to you, give him your undivided attention. Address your reply principally to him, but do not exclude the other board members.

8) Do not interrupt

A board member may be stating a problem for you to analyze. He will ask you a question when the time comes. Let him state the problem, and wait for the question.

9) Make sure you understand the question

Do not try to answer until you are sure what the question is. If it is not clear, restate it in your own words or ask the board member to clarify it for you. However, do not haggle about minor elements.

10) Reply promptly but not hastily

A common entry on oral board rating sheets is "candidate responded readily," or "candidate hesitated in replies." Respond as promptly and quickly as you can, but do not jump to a hasty, ill-considered answer.

11) Do not be peremptory in your answers

A brief answer is proper – but do not fire your answer back. That is a losing game from your point of view. The board member can probably ask questions much faster than you can answer them.

12) Do not try to create the answer you think the board member wants

He is interested in what kind of mind you have and how it works – not in playing games. Furthermore, he can usually spot this practice and will actually grade you down on it.

13) Do not switch sides in your reply merely to agree with a board member

Frequently, a member will take a contrary position merely to draw you out and to see if you are willing and able to defend your point of view. Do not start a debate, yet do not surrender a good position. If a position is worth taking, it is worth defending.

14) Do not be afraid to admit an error in judgment if you are shown to be wrong

The board knows that you are forced to reply without any opportunity for careful consideration. Your answer may be demonstrably wrong. If so, admit it and get on with the interview.

15) Do not dwell at length on your present job

The opening question may relate to your present assignment. Answer the question but do not go into an extended discussion. You are being examined for a *new* job, not your present one. As a matter of fact, try to phrase ALL your answers in terms of the job for which you are being examined.

Basis of Rating

Probably you will forget most of these "do's" and "don'ts" when you walk into the oral interview room. Even remembering them all will not ensure you a passing grade. Perhaps you did not have the qualifications in the first place. But remembering them will help you to put your best foot forward, without treading on the toes of the board members.

Rumor and popular opinion to the contrary notwithstanding, an oral board wants you to make the best appearance possible. They know you are under pressure – but they also want to see how you respond to it as a guide to what your reaction would be under the pressures of the job you seek. They will be influenced by the degree of poise you display, the personal traits you show and the manner in which you respond.

ABOUT THIS BOOK

This book contains tests divided into Examination Sections. Go through each test, answering every question in the margin. We have also attached a sample answer sheet at the back of the book that can be removed and used. At the end of each test look at the answer key and check your answers. On the ones you got wrong, look at the right answer choice and learn. Do not fill in the answers first. Do not memorize the questions and answers, but understand the answer and principles involved. On your test, the questions will likely be different from the samples. Questions are changed and new ones added. If you understand these past questions you should have success with any changes that arise. Tests may consist of several types of questions. We have additional books on each subject should more study be advisable or necessary for you. Finally, the more you study, the better prepared you will be. This book is intended to be the last thing you study before you walk into the examination room. Prior study of relevant texts is also recommended. NLC publishes some of these in our Fundamental Series. Knowledge and good sense are important factors in passing your exam. Good luck also helps. So now study this Passbook, absorb the material contained within and take that knowledge into the examination. Then do your best to pass that exam.

EXAMINATION SECTION

EXAMINATION SECTION

TEST 1

DIRECTIONS: Each question or incomplete statement is followed by several suggested answers or completions. Select the one that BEST answers the question or completes the statement. *PRINT THE LETTER OF THE CORRECT ANSWER IN THE SPACE AT THE RIGHT.*

1. The one of the following which is the PRINCIPAL medium of casework service is
    A. skilled diagnosis and realistic treatment planning
    B. personal communication or relationship established between the client and the worker
    C. agency organization in relation to program objectives
    D. the combined knowledge, skill, and attitude of the worker

    1._____

2. Treatment aimed at helping the client maintain his adaptive pattern is directed toward
    A. alleviating undue pressures in the client's everyday life and strengthening his emotional reactions to psychological pressure
    B. modifying the client's unrealistic life pattern by confronting him with explanations for his behavior
    C. assuming a passive role in order to avoid disturbing the client's adjustment
    D. working with those aspects of the client's problems which are related to environmental factors

    2._____

3. On account of the multi-faceted and dynamic nature of clients' problems, of the following, it is NECESSARY for the social worker to
    A. analyze the total problem before proceeding with treatment
    B. develop a comprehensive treatment plan which approaches the main aspects of the total problem
    C. separate the personality and behavioral aspects of the problem from the social setting
    D. select some part of the problem as the unit for work

    3._____

4. The one of the following which is the MOST important consideration in evaluating the ego strength of an angry, deprived, mistreated, frustrated, evasive client is the client's ability to
    A. verbalize his problems to someone
    B. redirect his anger towards an object
    C. form a relationship with an accepting worker
    D. hold a job

    4._____

2 (#1)

5. When a client is torn between choices that immobilize him or make his problem less manageable, the social worker should base his practice with the client on the following, with the EXCEPTION of
   A. identification of the client's problem
   B. persuading the client to act according to his instructions
   C. determination with the client of preferred approaches in dealing with the problem
   D. enabling the client to take constructive action to deal with the problem

5.____

6. Assume that a social worker reports that a mother with whom she is working claims that the school is discriminating against her children because she is a welfare recipient. Her children have a history of truancy and poor school achievement. The worker feels that the mother's assessment of the situation has some validity.
   Of the following, the BEST course of action for the worker to take is to
   A. support the mother's defense of her children and report the alleged discrimination by the school to the Board of Education
   B. inquire further into the reasons for the children's truancy and poor achievement with the children, the mother, and school officials
   C. explore with the mother her feelings about receiving public assistance, and encourage her to find a job so she won't need assistance
   D. disengage herself from her close involvement in this case since she has stopped being objective

6.____

7. A social worker has as a client a 17-year-old boy who is part of a group whose norm of behavior is cutting classes, frequent absenteeism, sexual promiscuity, and petty thievery. He wants to finish school and to grow up, but the present peer-group pressure militates against this, and he is damaging his values by following the group's norms.
   The social worker would be MOST helpful to this boy if, of the following, he takes the role of a
   A. mediator, to help support the boy against the demands of the group, and also to give him direct help in defending himself psychologically
   B. resource person, to refer the boy to a youth agency that would be able to work with the boy in his peer group
   C. interpreter, to help the boy realize the inappropriateness of his behavior in the peer group
   D. peer model, to help the boy identify with a young, successful person

7.____

8. A fifteen-year-old boy has been referred to a social worker with a history of arrests for repeated acts of minor delinquency, suspension from school for truancy, and a hostile attitude towards treatment. He is financially supported by his parents, but they seem to have stopped giving him emotional support and say that he is uncontrollable.
The boy's interests would be served BEST if, of the following, the social worker's role were that of
   A. psychosocial counselor using traditional insight development
   B. educator in teaching the boy the skills he would need to succeed
   C. catalyst in family therapy, to help the boy and his parents handle their feelings and the reality problems constructively
   D. crisis intervenor, taking an assertive role to give direction and specific help

9. The one of the following which is a COMMON error made by new social workers who are beginning to find out about the influence of unconscious desires and emotions on human behavior is to
   A. probe the client unnecessarily
   B. become over-assured that they can solve the client's problem
   C. slow up the pace of the interview
   D. look for the proper treatment method based on the client's neuroses

10. Although we can judge statements about objective verifiable matters to be true or false, we are not similarly justified in passing judgment on subjective attitudes.
Of the following, this statement BEST explains the rationale behind the social work principle of
   A. empathy   B. abreaction
   C. non-judgmentality   D. confidentiality

11. The one of the following which BEST describes the meaning of ambivalence in social work is: The
   A. social worker refrains from imposing his moral judgments on the client
   B. supervisor assists the worker in understanding the psychological causes for the client's behavior
   C. client is seeking someone who will understand the subjective reasons for his behavior
   D. client has conflicting interests, desires, and emotions

12. The CORRECT definition of the term *acceptance* as used in social work is as follows:
   A. A decision made at intake to accept the client as a case for the agency to handle
   B. The concept of a positive and active understanding by the worker of the feelings a client expresses through his behavior
   C. The concept that the worker does not pass judgment on the client's behavior
   D. Communication to the client that the worker does not condone and accept his antisocial behavior

13. Psychiatrists are usually concerned with the total functioning and integration of the human personality.
    Of the following, social workers USUALLY concentrate on
    A. the same thing but for shorter periods of time
    B. the same thing but without prescribing medication
    C. helping the client to deal with the presenting problem
    D. making the proper referrals to assist the client in dealing with his problem

14. The one of the following which is a DESCRIPTIVE term for a client who is resistive, breaks appointments, withholds information, beclouds issues, related to others in a primitive, often distorted fashion, and acts out his wishes and conflicts in his contact with the worker is
    A. psychotic   B. manic depressive
    C. paranoid schizophrenic   D. character disorder

15. The one of the following which is a MAJOR reason why it is so difficult for social workers to exert influence on social policy is:
    A. Social workers are trained to implement existing policies, not to change those that are unworkable
    B. Those who make policy are influenced by numerous forces, persons, values, and aspirations, not all of which relate directly to the policy decisions to be made
    C. As a result of the heavy concentration on casework in the graduate schools, most social workers put more emphasis on working with individuals, rather than on social policy
    D. Psychological and psychiatric concepts are disputed by experts in the field, so that it is difficult to diagnose motives

16. The one of the following which is the BEST explanation of the rationale of *crisis intervention* as a treatment method is:
    A. A little help, rationally directed and purposefully focused at an extremely critical time in the client's life, can be more effective than more extensive help given during a less critical period
    B. Because clients are more likely to react precipitously at times of crisis, social workers must give particular emphasis at such times to providing direct and aggressive advice and assistance
    C. The social worker should make full use of the client's vulnerable emotional state at a time of crisis in order to bring him face to face with his defense mechanisms and with the realities of life
    D. The client's urgent need for emotional support at times of crisis should be used by the social worker at such times to gain the client's confidence and trust

17. In establishing contact with a new, unfamiliar group, of the following, the group worker's usual FIRST action should be to
    A. discuss the sponsoring agency and its function
    B. give special attention to the less aggressive members
    C. reinforce the authority of the natural group leader
    D. approach the group at their own level of language and interests

18. If a group worker should become aware that some members of his group feel resentful toward him, of the following, it would GENERALLY be advisable for the worker to
    A. make a special effort to please the resentful members
    B. offer to resign from leadership of the group
    C. attempt to convey to the resentful members his own attitude of acceptance of them
    D. enlist the support of other group members to convince the resentful ones of his good intentions

19. Assume that, during the sixth weekly session of activity group therapy with a group of adolescent boys, they engage in horseplay, use obscene language, and become quite uncontrollable.
    Of the following, it can SAFELY be concluded that the
    A. boys are testing the worker to learn his limits of tolerance
    B. worker's status as the group leader is being seriously challenged
    C. composition of the group should be changed
    D. worker should end the session and dismiss the boys

20. Of the following, the role of the group worker at meetings of a group which has its own officers is to
    A. withdraw from the activities of the group
    B. make decisions for the group if required
    C. clarify issues and teach skills when necessary
    D. handle hostile or aggressive members

21. Schizophrenia in children USUALLY becomes manifest
    A. during the latency period
    B. during adolescence only
    C. when the mother has a history of schizophrenia
    D. during early childhood or adolescence

22. Sickle cell anemia is a blood disease MOST commonly found in children whose parents are
    A. Caucasian   B. interracial
    B. black or Latin American D. oriental

23. A decline in hearing and vision takes place in healthy persons during the period BEGINNING at age
    A. 30   B. 40   C. 50   D. 60

24. The MOST common complaint made by psychiatric patients is concerned with
    A. depression   B. panic   C. insomnia   D. fatigue

25. The one of the following which is *most likely* to cause the reappearance in old age of a previously compensated neurosis is
    A. decrease in social status, loss of persons and possessions or presence of injuries and illnesses
    B. decrease in sensory and cognitive capacities resulting in poor reality testing
    C. cerebro-arteriosclerosis or other cerebrovascular disturbance
    D. decrease in financial resources, resulting in heightened anxiety

25._____

KEY (CORRECT ANSWERS)

1. B
2. A
3. D
4. C
5. B

6. B
7. A
8. C
9. A
10. C

11. D
12. B
13. C
14. D
15. B

16. A
17. D
18. C
19. A
20. C

21. D
22. C
23. B
24. A
25. A

TEST 2

DIRECTIONS: Each question or incomplete statement is followed by several suggested answers or completions. Select the one that BEST answers the question or completes the statement. *PRINT THE LETTER OF THE CORRECT ANSWER IN THE SPACE AT THE RIGHT.*

1. Of the following, group approaches are COMMONLY used for
    A. encounter, discussion, training, and administration
    B. education, counseling, therapy, and recreation
    C. counseling, recreation, catharsis, and crisis intervention
    D. counseling, leadership, administration, and training

    1._____

2. The purposes of group counseling are the following, with the EXCEPTION of
    A. avoidance of treating pathology as such
    B. helping clients attain a better level of functioning
    C. modifying social and familial problems
    D. resolving intra-psychic conflicts

    2._____

3. The separation of public assistance recipients into categories had its origins in the
    A. Elizabethan poor law
    B. numerous amendments to the Social Security Act
    C. legislation of the Massachusetts Bay Colony
    D. Social Security Act of 1935

    3._____

4. The one of the following which is the FIRST form of social insurance to be widely developed in the United States is
    A. workmen's compensation or industrial accident insurance
    B. unemployment insurance programs
    C. temporary disability insurance
    D. old age insurance for industrial workers

    4._____

5. The doctrine of less eligibility, which has been considered over the years as a policy for public assistance programs, means most nearly that
    A. grants should always be below subsistence level in order to give recipients an incentive to seek employment
    B. eligibility for public assistance should be established on the basis of a limited number of basic budgetary needs
    C. income derived from public assistance benefits should not exceed the amount earned by the lowest paid independent worker in the community
    D. categories of need should be established in each community and ranked in order of priority in order to determine eligibility for assistance

    5._____

6. Social insurance programs such as OASDHI and unemployment insurance have been CRITICIZED widely because, of the following,
   a. there is an inherent conflict between the intent to prevent poverty on the one hand, and wage-relatedness of the programs on the other
   b. there is no relationship between the amount or the benefits and differences in cost of living in various localities within a state
   c. the programs do not include review of personal and family problems
   d. a large percentage of the grants go to persons who are otherwise financially able to support themselves

7. The one of the following which would be the basis of a family allowance plan SIMILAR to programs in effect in Canada and France is:
   a. Family size, for all needy families with minor children whose current annual income is below specified levels
   b. The total number of persons in the household, including all adults except those receiving social security benefits
   c. The number of minor children, available to all families and requiring no means test
   d. Income level, available to all families with minor children

8. A MAJOR criticism of social and health programs as they exist today has been the tendency towards a *problem focus* rather than a *social goals* approach.
   Of the following, this approach has resulted in
   a. a lack of an integrated, systematic development of programs that deal adequately with social and health problems
   b. excessive expenditures for the social and health problems that have received the most attention, at the expense of other equally serious problems
   c. a federal and nationwide approach rather than the more desirable *geographic approach*, which would bring delivery of services closer to the people
   d. the development of legislation which shows little evidence of recognition of the contributions that could be made by social planners

9. A striking feature of American culture is its tendency to identify standards of personal excellence with competitive occupational achievement.
   The one of the following which is the CONSEQUENCE of this feature for those unable to make one's own living through work is to
   a. increase incentive to find a productive job
   b. lower the individual's feeling of self-worth and generate a feeling of powerlessness
   c. give the individual a need to control the environment
   d. encourage increased educational attainment

10. Of the following, the objectives and curriculum content of graduate schools of social work today GENERALLY indicate an *increased* emphasis on
    a. prevention and institutional change in addition to treatment
    b. knowledge of individual personality factors and treatment methods
    c. the separate methods and goals of classroom study and field work
    d. the use of the one-to-one instructor-student relationship for both classroom study and field work

11. At present, there is a general consensus among social welfare educators and administrators that not every job requires a professional social worker with a master's degree in social work.
    The one of the following which is the MOST important reason for this viewpoint is that personnel with lower educational qualifications can
    a. be used as a valuable temporary expedient for jobs that would otherwise remain unfilled
    b. perform certain social work tasks as well or even better than workers with master's degrees
    c. gain experience that will spur them on to attend a graduate school of social work in order to obtain the degree
    d. be used to reduce substantially personnel costs in public and private social work agencies

12. In an era of rapid change, of the following, the REAL test of the social work profession is to
    a. meet constructively the demands of that change
    b. hold to its traditional practices
    c. abandon its methods for new approaches
    d. wait to see what happens to other professions

13. The psychologist who is USUALLY associated with a theory of self-psychology which has as its basic concept the assertion that a man has a tendency to actualize himself, i.e., to maintain and improve himself, is
    A. Karl Jung
    B. Sigmund Freud
    C. B.F. Skinner
    D. Carl Rogers

14. Of the types of mental breakdown listed below, the disorder that ordinarily occurs at the MOST advanced age is
    A. cerebral arteriosclerosis
    B. neurasthenia
    C. dementia praecox
    D. paresis

15. Principles of crisis intervention in social casework have been derived LARGELY from the theoretical formulations of
    a. Harry Stack Sullivan and Clara Thompson
    b. August P. Hollingshead and Frederick C. Redlich
    c. Otto Rank and Jessie Taft
    d. Erich Lindemann and Gerald Caplan

16. Of the following, the MOST important reason that those responsible for the care of a child in placement should *never* depreciate the child's natural parents or the home from which he came is that the
    a. child's self-esteem depends on how he feels about his natural parents and his previous experiences
    b. natural parents may have been incapable of being adequate parents
    c. child may feel the substitute parents are jealous of his natural parents
    d. child will be forced into the position of defending his natural parents and will resent the substitute parents

16._____

17. Although day care was originally established mainly as a social service for working mothers, it has been found that, of the following,
    a. working mothers of physically and mentally handicapped children do not benefit from day care facilities
    b. most working mothers would prefer to leave their children with friends or relatives rather than at a day care center
    c. it would be economically feasible and beneficial for communities to establish day care centers which would be available to all mothers in the community
    d. day care can also be an educational experience for a child and be helpful in the development of peer relationships

17._____

18. Research studies of language development in young children have shown that, of the following,
    a. the multiple mothering of children in a large family retards language development
    b. language retardation in otherwise normal children is usually related to inadequate language stimulation
    c. language retardation is always associated with slow motor development
    d. children are usually slow in learning to talk when more than one language is spoken in the home

18._____

19. The *battered child syndrome* is reported to be one of the most difficult problems facing health officials. When a worker knows of a case of a child being severely physically abused, of the following, he SHOULD
    a. get psychiatric consultation to understand the parents' motives
    b. advise the child to stay away from the parents
    c. help the parents to see what they're doing is wrong
    d. report the case to child protective authorities

19._____

20. The one of the following which is a *psychological principle* which can BEST be described as a situation in which an individual experiences some ambivalence and indecisiveness in choosing one or more desired objects or goals is
    A. task-orientation   B. conflict
    C. apathy   D. projection

20._____

21. The *treatment method* which allows or encourages the client to express his charged feelings around a pressing emotional need is known as
    A. exploring
    B. synthesizing
    C. catharsis
    D. ventilating

22. The *emotional release* that results from recall of a previously forgotten painful experience is known as
    A. introjection
    B. abreaction
    C. sublimation
    D. free association

23. The *action* whereby an individual directs his aggression against an innocent bystander rather than expressing it against the source of his difficulties, is called
    A. displacement
    B. projection
    C. introjection
    D. abreaction

24. An *attempt* to attribute emotionally caused behavior to reasonable factors MORE acceptable to the individual is known as
    A. projection
    B. rationalization
    C. introjection
    D. free association

25. The UNCONSCIOUS *application* of elements of the experiences in a former relationship to a new relationship is known as
    A. projection
    B. abreaction
    C. transference
    D. sublimation

KEY (CORRECT ANSWERS)

1. B	11. B
2. D	12. A
3. A	13. D
4. A	14. A
5. C	15. D
6. A	16. A
7. C	17. D
8. A	18. B
9. B	19. D
10. A	20. B

21. D
22. B
23. A
24. B
25. C

EXAMINATION SECTION
TEST 1

DIRECTIONS: Each question or incomplete statement is followed by several suggested answers or completions. Select the one that BEST answers the question or completes the statement. *PRINT THE LETTER OF THE CORRECT ANSWER IN THE SPACE AT THE RIGHT.*

1. Frequent reference has been made to a *safety net* of basic social services by which the needy would be maintained in spite of budget cuts.
   Which of the following pairs of items is NOT included in the term *safety net*?

   A. Social Security and SSI
   B. Unemployment Insurance and Workers' Compensation
   C. Medicaid and Municipal Health Services
   D. Home Relief and AFDC

   1.____

2. As a supervisor in an office that provides direct services to clients, your case managers and team supervisors are constantly under stress caused by the necessity to make decisions, particularly those which may permanently change clients' lives, as in cases involving adoption, institutionalization, or removal of a child from home.
   Of the following, you can BEST assist staff in reducing these client-related pressures by

   A. providing them with a clear understanding of authority and specific guidelines regarding who is to make decisions under particular circumstances
   B. assuring them that the Agency head has ultimate responsibility for critical decisions affecting clients' lives
   C. helping them understand that clients have the right to self-determination and are largely responsible for making critical decisions
   D. training them to be realistic and objective, thus relieving them of the burden of responsibility for unfavorable client-related decisions

   2.____

3. Of the following, the MOST important reason why group methods are effective in working with disadvantaged clients is that these clients

   A. are less likely to express feelings of anger in a group setting
   B. may resent discussing any personal problems with individual workers
   C. are more likely to share information about themselves in a group setting
   D. usually seek the approval of others for their actions

   3.____

4. As a Supervisor II responsible for the operation of three units, you find that one of your units has a particularly high rate of turnover. Clients are complaining that their cases have been mismanaged because of the staff shortage. Of the following, the FIRST action you should take in this situation is to

   A. reassign caseworkers so that all units have coverage
   B. try to determine why workers are unwilling to work in this unit
   C. ask for additional help from your supervisor
   D. handle some of the caseload yourself

   4.____

13

5. A new Supervisor I from another Human Resources Administration (HRA) component has been assigned to your office. The LEAST useful way to orient him to the job is to

   A. set up a regular conference schedule to discuss any questions and problems that arise
   B. give him all procedures to read and review them with him
   C. phase in the workload gradually within an agreed upon time frame
   D. ask him to work independently and make independent decisions as much as possible

6. You find that there is an important procedural error in a memo which you distributed to your staff several days ago. The BEST approach for you to take at this time is to

   A. send a corrected memo to the staff, indicating what prior error was made
   B. send a corrected memo to the staff without mentioning the prior error
   C. tell the staff about the error at the next monthly staff meeting
   D. place the corrected memo on the office bulletin board

7. The primary responsibility of a Liaison and Adjustment Unit in an Income Maintenance Center is to assist in resolving clients' appeals of Departmental decisions affecting their eligibility for public assistance.
   In order to ensure that the unit's decisions are in compliance with agency and governmental regulations, it is MOST important for the supervisor of the unit to

   A. review all appeals for Fair Hearings prior to assignment to subordinates
   B. routinely hold staff meetings to discuss the unit's performance
   C. regularly review agency rules and governmental laws regarding public assistance
   D. maintain records in order to insure equalization of the work flow

8. Your supervisor asks you, a Supervisor II, about the status of the response to a letter from a public official concerning a client's case. When you ask the subordinate who was assigned to prepare the response to give you the letter, the subordinate denies that it was given to him. You are certain that the subordinate has the letter, but is withholding it because the response has not yet been prepared.
   Of the following, in order to secure the letter from the subordinate, you should FIRST

   A. accuse the subordinate of lying and demand that the letter be given to you immediately
   B. say that you would consider it a personal favor if the subordinate would find the letter
   C. continue to question the subordinate until he admits to having been given the letter
   D. offer a face-saving solution, such as asking the subordinate to look again for the letter

9. As a Supervisor II, you have been assigned to write a few paragraphs to be included in the agency's annual report, describing the Department of Social Services this year as compared to last year.
   Which of the following elements basic to the agency is LEAST likely to have changed since last year?

   A. Mission   B. Structure   C. Technology   D. Personnel

10. A female client calls you, a Supervisor II, to complain that a male caseworker employed by a vendor agency has requested that she have sexual relations with him in return for the help he has given to her.
    In this situation, you should FIRST tell the client that

    A. you will call the head of the vendor agency and have the caseworker dismissed
    B. she must submit her complaint in writing as soon as possible so that you can investigate the situation
    C. you will immediately call the head of the vendor agency and report her complaint
    D. she must report this complaint to the Office of the Inspector General

11. As a Supervisor II, you have been informed that a grievance has been filed against you, accusing you of assigning a subordinate to out-of-title tasks.
    Of the following, the BEST approach for you to take is to

    A. waive the grievance so that it will proceed to a Step II hearing
    B. immediately change the subordinate's assignment to avoid future problems
    C. respond to the grievance, giving appropriate reasons for the assignment
    D. review the job description to ensure that the subordinate's tasks are not out-of-title

12. Assume you are a Supervisor II in a division that requires supervisory staff from the various units to discuss work related issues. You notice that two of your unit supervisors refuse to talk to each other.
    The BEST action to take in this situation is to

    A. ask one of your other supervisors what he thinks is the cause of the situation
    B. call a staff meeting to explain the importance of harmony among the staff
    C. ignore the situation and hope that in time their relationship will improve
    D. discuss ways to resolve the problem with the two supervisors

13. Assume that you are a Supervisor II who has recently been assigned to a new office. One of your subordinates is performing below standard in several of his assigned tasks. A review of the personnel folder does not indicate any previous problems.
    Of the following, the LEAST appropriate action for you to take is to

    A. hold a series of regularly scheduled conferences with the subordinate to discuss work problems
    B. advise the subordinate to improve his performance or request a transfer
    C. discuss the matter with your supervisor in order to develop a plan for supervision and performance review
    D. bring the matter to the subordinate's attention to develop a mutual understanding of the problem

14. Which of the following is NOT a correct statement about agency group training programs in a public service welfare agency?

    A. Training sessions continue for an indefinite period of time.
    B. Group training sessions are planned for designated personnel.
    C. Training groups are organized formally through administrative planning.
    D. Group training is task-centered and aimed toward accomplishing specific educational goals.

15. As a Supervisor II, you have received an assignment with an instructional sheet regarding a new procedure in Family and Adult Services. You do not quite understand part of the instructions.
    The BEST way to handle this is to

    A. try to carry out the assignment in accordance with your interpretation of the instructions
    B. interpret the assignment according to the previous procedure
    C. explain to your workers that you are not responsible for the instructions
    D. ask your supervisor to clarify the instructions for you

16. You are a Supervisor II responsible for a unit that is required to handle a large number of emergency cases in addition to the regular caseload.
    In order to prevent the continual assignment of emergency cases to the same workers, it is GOOD practice to

    A. assign cases in rotation
    B. redistribute cases to equalize the caseload
    C. designate a daily emergency worker
    D. interpret eligibility requirements more strictly

17. You are a Supervisor II who often holds group meetings with your staff to discuss problem cases.
    This method of supervision is LEAST valuable for

    A. providing an effective way of disseminating information
    B. dealing with individual needs for knowledge and skills
    C. involving staff in unit decision-making
    D. learning from the supervisor and each other

18. A caseworker in a program for which you are responsible advises you that she and her supervisor, a Supervisor I, have a disagreement over what services should be provided in a specific case.
    As the Supervisor II, the FIRST action you should take is to

    A. tell the caseworker to follow the advice of the Supervisor I
    B. meet with both the caseworker and the Supervisor I to hear their arguments
    C. review the case in question to become familiar with the material
    D. tell the caseworker and the supervisor to settle the matter between themselves

19. You are a case supervisor in a General Social Services district office. Your director informs you that a recent audit report indicates that the case managers in your district are making fewer than the required number of field visits per field day. It occurs to you that a substantial number of such visits are probably not being recorded on the Field Activity Reports.
    The FIRST step you should take in this situation is to

    A. review a random sample of Field Activity Reports and case records
    B. write a memorandum to the team supervisor requesting that all field visits be properly documented
    C. call a meeting of all case managers and the team supervisor to discuss the field visit procedure
    D. advise the director that you feel the audit is based on incomplete information

20. A Supervisor I under your direction tells you that he regularly cannot account for one of his caseworker's whereabouts, and his frequent absence causes problems in the assignment of cases and telephone coverage.
In this situation, you should FIRST

    A. tell the supervisor to have the absent worker account for his time
    B. ask the supervisor what action he has taken to have the worker document his time
    C. hold a meeting with the worker and the supervisor to discuss the problem
    D. tell the supervisor to meet with the unit as a whole to discuss the problem

21. You are the Supervisor II in a General Social Services district office. The director of the office has asked you to determine why a particular unit consistently submits its work late. The MOST effective step to take FIRST is to

    A. inform the unit supervisor that he will receive a negative performance evaluation if the situation does not improve
    B. inform the unit supervisor that you have analyzed the situation and expect him to carry out the solution you offer
    C. ask the unit supervisor to assess the situation and take corrective action
    D. meet with the unit supervisor and mutually discuss the problems and what should be done to resolve them

22. As a Supervisor II, you have submitted a memo to your supervisor requesting a conference to discuss the performance of a Supervisor I under your supervision. The memo states that the Supervisor I has a good working relationship with her staff; however, she tends to interpret agency policy too liberally and shows poor administrative skills by missing some deadlines and not keeping proper controls.
Which of the following steps should NOT be taken in order to prepare for this conference with your Supervisor III?

    A. Collect and review all your notes regarding the Supervisor I's prior performance.
    B. Outline your agenda so that you will have sufficient time to discuss the situation.
    C. Tell the Supervisor I that you will be discussing her performance with your supervisor.
    D. Clearly define objectives which will focus on improving the Supervisor I's performance.

23. Assume that you are training and guiding a new supervisor who has spent a number of years as a caseworker and who says that she feels more comfortable with a participatory rather than a directive leadership style, since participation more closely reflects her previous experience.
You should advise her that, of the following, use of the participatory style is LEAST effective when

    A. staff has information which bears on the issue
    B. participants derive ego-satisfaction from the tasks
    C. the supervisor and workers have different goals and interests
    D. tasks are ambiguous and complex

24. You are a Supervisor II assigned to the personnel section of your agency. A friend in one of the divisions, whom you know to be an excellent employee, requests that you recommend to his supervisor or director that he be considered for promotion.
The BEST course of action for you to take is to

    A. *comply* with his request since he is a friend of yours
    B. *comply* with his request because you know his director is noted for never recommending employees for promotion
    C. *reject* the request and inform the director of the program of your friend's unethical behavior
    D. *reject* the request since only his supervisor or the director of the program can submit such a recommendation

25. As a Supervisor II, you are about to plan an informational meeting with your staff regarding a new reporting form. Which of the following should NOT be included in preparing for this meeting?

    A. Defining the purpose clearly
    B. Preparing a written agenda
    C. Inviting all levels of staff
    D. Allowing time for questions and answers

KEY (CORRECT ANSWERS)

1.	B	11.	C
2.	A	12.	D
3.	C	13.	B
4.	B	14.	A
5.	D	15.	D
6.	A	16.	C/A
7.	C	17.	B
8.	D	18.	C
9.	A	19.	A
10.	C	20.	B

21. D
22. C
23. C
24. D
25. C

TEST 2

DIRECTIONS: Each question or incomplete statement is followed by several suggested answers or completions. Select the one that BEST answers the question or completes the statement. *PRINT THE LETTER OF THE CORRECT ANSWER IN THE SPACE AT THE RIGHT.*

1. During a supervisory conference with your unit supervisors, you learn that on the previous day one of the workers in your program gave some confidential case information to an investigative reporter.
   As the Supervisor II, of the following, the FIRST action for you to take in this situation is to

   A. inform the director about the incident
   B. advise the Office of the Inspector General
   C. ask the worker the details of what occurred
   D. assign a new worker to the case

   1.____

2. You have been asked by your director to prepare a memo to the staff describing a new procedure.
   In writing the memo, of the following, the MOST important thing to keep in mind is that the

   A. memo should include all data the staff will need in order to implement the procedure
   B. language of the memo should be as direct as possible
   C. staff should be informed that they are expected to act on the content of the memo
   D. tone of the memo should be polite and encouraging so that the staff will respond favorably

   2.____

3. Mr. Smith, a Supervisor I under your supervision, gives you a memorandum requesting approval to issue emergency clothing funds to one of his clients. After reviewing the request, you find that Mr. Smith has failed to include essential client information in the memorandum. Because of the client's emergency need, of the following, the BEST approach for you to take in this situation is to

   A. approve the request and set aside time to work with Mr. Smith on memo preparation
   B. ask pertinent questions to get the information you need to approve the request
   C. ask Mr. Smith to review the case and to revise the memo to include the additional information
   D. deny the request due to insufficient information

   3.____

4. As a Supervisor II in a General Social Services district office, you have received a telephone call from a neighborhood resident who informs you that she has just witnessed the man next door physically abusing his wife and children and shouting obscenities at them. When assigning the case, of the following, you should advise the Supervisor I and caseworker to

   A. call the police so that they can be at the home when the caseworker arrives
   B. call the wife and give her the address of the battered women's shelter
   C. make an immediate home visit to assess the case and develop a service plan
   D. assist the wife in securing an order of protection for her and the children

   4.____

19

5. Because of staff shortages, a Supervisor II assigns the unit's best worker to handle occasional difficult cases in addition to the regular caseload. The other workers in the unit are not assigned these difficult cases.
This method of making assignments is

   A. *advisable* because staff shortages must be overcome
   B. *advisable* because this worker will handle the difficult cases better
   C. *inadvisable* because of the *equal work for equal pay* concept
   D. *inadvisable* because the worker will be overburdened

6. As a Supervisor II in a General Social Services district office, you have been requested to develop a resource inventory for your district.
Such an inventory is LEAST valuable in identifying

   A. providers of special services in your district's community
   B. service needs not being met in your district
   C. service definitions to be used by service providers in your district
   D. alternate funding sources to meet special service needs in your district

7. During the weekly conference with your unit supervisors, you tell them that the workers are not completing the new required forms on time, thus delaying provision of services to clients. The supervisors state that the new forms are very complicated and that the workers need training in filling them out.
In order to determine whether training is necessary, as the Supervisor II, of the following, the LEAST appropriate action you should take would be to

   A. revise the form to make it more simple
   B. find out whether the workers know how to complete the form
   C. study the form to see if the instructions are clear
   D. discuss with the supervisors other possible reasons for the workers' poor performance

8. As the field supervisor for a program in Special Services for Children, you have become aware that one of the provisional caseworkers has been arriving late, leaving early, and, on occasion, failing to advise anyone of his whereabouts during working hours.
Since you know that the worker has been effective in handling client problems, the MOST appropriate step for you to take is to

   A. write a report of the situation and submit it to the director
   B. advise the worker that he faces disciplinary action
   C. call the worker in for a conference to discuss the problem
   D. consider possible transfer to another program within the agency

9. A Supervisor I newly assigned to your unit in an Income Maintenance Center has a history of closing cases whenever the eligibility decision is a close one. He boasts about how much money he saves the government with each case closed. However, many of his closed cases have had to be reopened on appeal; and, in several instances, hasty closings have resulted in the breakup of families and the placement of children.
Of the following, the approach MOST likely to modify this supervisor's views would be to

   A. appeal to his humanity so that he will have a greater empathy for his clients
   B. order him to fully document all reasons for future closings

C. meet with his unit and reprimand them for closing eligible cases
D. discuss with him the actual cost to the government, such as the expense of child placement

10. In the course of reviewing case records being sent to you for your approval, you find that many errors are being made in relation to a certain procedure.
    The FIRST step for you to take in this situation is to

    A. send a memo to staff asking them to review the procedure
    B. bring the situation to the attention of the director
    C. call your subordinate supervisors together to discuss the problem
    D. develop a training program to review the procedure

11. You are a Supervisor II responsible for keeping accurate records of the status of the cases being handled by the units under your supervision.
    Of the following, the types of statistical controls which would be LEAST helpful to you are those that

    A. help you to spot trouble early
    B. analyze every component of your supervisors' tasks
    C. enable you to pinpoint cases that are exceptions to the norm
    D. provide you with statistical comparisons among units performing the same tasks

12. Assume that you are a Supervisor II in a field office. One of your Supervisor I's tells you that the unit was ordered by the Deputy Director, who is a Supervisor III, to perform a task in a way which is clearly not in accordance with standard procedure.
    In this situation, the BEST action for you to take is to

    A. discuss the matter with the Supervisor III to learn why the order was given
    B. tell the Supervisor I to disregard the order and continue following standard procedure
    C. report to the director that the Supervisor III is interfering with your supervision of your unit
    D. tell the Supervisor I to obey the order for now but to revert to standard procedure if trouble arises

13. As a Supervisor II in the Office of Staff Development and Training, you supervise five field instructors (Supervisor I's). Two of the five are frequently late in submitting their weekly statistical reports.
    The MOST appropriate action for you to take FIRST in this situation is to

    A. meet with both supervisors for a three-way discussion of the problem
    B. distribute a memo to all staff, stressing the need to complete all reports on time
    C. discuss the problem at your next supervisory meeting
    D. meet individually with each of the two supervisors involved

14. During the past two months, one of your most competent supervisors has done less effective work and appears listless and preoccupied.
    In order to get him back to his former high level of productivity, which of the following steps should you take FIRST?

    A. Reassign a substantial portion of his work, to take some of the pressure off him.
    B. Work with him to plan his day so he can more effectively use his time.

4 (#2)

C. Tell the supervisor you have observed that he appears to be preoccupied lately and ask him what is wrong.
D. Tell the supervisor that he should go on sick leave until he feels better.

Questions 15-18.

DIRECTIONS: Questions 15 through 18 are to be answered SOLELY on the basis of the information contained in the chart below.

PUBLIC ASSISTANCE CASES AND PERSONS
BY COMMUNITY DISTRICT (CD)
DECEMBER 2002, SEPTEMBER 2004, AND SEPTEMBER 2005

CD	Number of Cases			Number of Persons			Percent Change			
							12/02 to 9/05		9/04 to 9/05	
	12/02	9/04	9/05	12/04	9/04	9/05	Cases	Persons	Cases	Persons
1	4088	4071	4095	11360	11062	10845	0.2	-4.5	0.6	-2.0
2	1135	1130	1175	2817	2660	2757	3.5	-2.1	4.0	3.6
3	3033	3189	3230	8267	8355	8359	6.5	1.1	1.3	0.0
4	2202	2314	2370	6144	6212	6243	7.6	1.6	2.4	0.5
5	463	403	918	1207	970	2305	98.3	91.0	127.8	137.6
6	416	416	42	879	867	870	1.2	-1.0	1.2	0.3
7	1584	1534	1472	3977	3697	3427	-7.1	-13.8	-4.0	-7.3
8	1056	1055	107	2726	2586	2511	2.1	-7.9	2.2	-2.9
9	1820	1888	1968	5017	5025	5040	8.1	0.5	4.2	0.3
10	2007	1914	1996	5746	5234	5247	-0.5	-8.7	4.3	0.2
11	484	414	408	1267	1018	1000	-15.7	-21.1	-1.4	-1.8
12	9357	8819	9001	25608	22937	22857	-3.8	-10.7	2.1	-0.3
13	2420	2237	2237	6465	5577	5495	-7.6	-15.0	0.0	-1.5
14	3780	3880	4007	11408	11350	11670	6.0	2.3	3.3	2.8
Total	35807	35031	36167	98251	92329	93267	1.0	-5.1	3.2	1.0

15. The community district that had the LARGEST decrease in the number of cases from 12/02 to 9/05 is

A. CD7   B. CD11   C. CD12   D. CD13

16. Which one of the following statements is MOST supported by the chart?

A. CD5 had the largest increase in the number of cases from 12/02 to 9/04.
B. CD5 had the largest decrease in the number of persons on public assistance from 9/04 to 9/05.
C. CD7 had the largest decrease in the number of persons on public assistance from 12/02 to 9/05.
D. CD12 had more than five times the number of cases as CD9 in 9/05.

17. Borough-wide, the total number of persons on public assistance decreased from 12/02 to 9/04 and increased from 9/04 to 9/05.
Which one of the following includes all the community districts which followed this same pattern of change?

A. CD2, CD5, CD6, CD10, CD14
B. CD2, CD5, CD6, CD7, CD14
C. CD2, CD5, CD6, CD12, CD14
D. GD1, CD5, CD5, CD11, CD12

18. During the periods 12/02 to 9/04 and 9/04 to 9/05, how many community districts showed continual increases in both the number of cases and the number of persons receiving public assistance?

A. 2 B. 3 C. 4 D. 5

Questions 19-22.

DIRECTIONS: Questions 19 through 22 are to be answered SOLELY on the basis of the information contained in the following passage.

The Commissioner and, with the approval of the Commissioner, the Inspectors General and any person under the supervision of the Commissioner or Inspectors General may require any officer or employee of the city to answer questions concerning any matter related to the performance of his or her official duties or any person dealing with the city concerning such dealings with the city, after first being advised that neither their statements nor any information or evidence derived therefrom will be used against them in a subsequent criminal prosecution other than for perjury or contempt arising from such testimony. The refusal of an officer or employee to answer questions on the condition described in this paragraph shall constitute cause for removal from office or employment or other appropriate penalty.

Every officer or employee of the city shall cooperate fully with the Commissioner and the Inspectors General. Interference with or obstruction of an investigation conducted by the Commissioner or an Inspector General shall constitute cause for removal from office or employment or other appropriate penalty.

Every officer and employee of the city shall have the affirmative obligation to report, directly and without undue delay, to the Commissioner or an Inspector General any and all information concerning conduct which they know or should reasonably know to involve corrupt or other criminal activity or conflict of interest, (1) by another city officer or employee, which concerns his or her office or employment, or (2) by persons dealing with the city, which concerns their dealings with the city. The knowing failure of any officer or employee to report as required above shall constitute cause for removal from office or employment or other appropriate penalty.

19. According to the above passage, if a city employee has information concerning criminal wrongdoing by her supervisor in his work with a private agency, she should FIRST

A. speak with her supervisor about the matter
B. inform the Inspector General of the information she has
C. explore the matter further to try to uncover more evidence
D. speak to her co-workers to determine whether her suspicions are valid

20. Of the following, the passage is MOST concerned with

    A. preventing corrupt or other criminal activity or conflicts of interest in city dealings
    B. establishing what constitutes corrupt or criminal activities by city employees
    C. establishing guidelines for removing city employees from office who do not assist the Inspector General
    D. city employees' responsibilities regarding investigations conducted by the Office of the Inspector General

21. Based on the above passage, it is NOT always necessary to report which one of the following to the Inspector General?

    A. A city employee who accepts a gift from a private business
    B. A private agency whose work for the city presents a conflict of interest
    C. A private vendor who offers a city employee special favors if awarded a city contract
    D. A city employee who conducts private business during his city working hours

22. Of the following, the above passage does NOT discuss the type of penalty a city employee might receive for

    A. intentionally giving misleading answers to questions asked by the Inspector General
    B. criminal actions he committed and which subsequently are uncovered by an investigation of the Inspector General
    C. interfering with an investigation being conducted by the Inspector General
    D. delaying to report corrupt activity to the Inspector General

Questions 23-25.

DIRECTIONS: Questions 23 through 25 are to be answered SOLELY on the basis of the information contained in the following passage.

In 2009, funding for the Older Americans Act programs will be cut by 10% from the 2008 funding levels. There will be 4.6 million dollars less in funds available for congregate and home-delivered meals, employment, and social services for the city's 1.2 million elderly residents. Funding for the Title V Senior Community Services Employment program would be effectively discontinued, resulting in the loss of jobs for 684 elderly persons working in nutrition sites for the elderly, senior centers, day care centers, and hospitals. This job loss would add to the almost 800 jobs in N.Y.C. defunded by the elimination of the Job Opportunity Program. Reductions in the Title IIIC Nutrition and Commodity Foods/cash in lieu programs will jeopardize the delivery of over 500,000 congregate and home-delivered meals annually, and the operation of seven senior citizens centers. Title IIIB services, which include home care, escort, shopping, and transportation services, will be spared in 2009 because of the availability of prior year funds, but will be reduced by nearly one million dollars in 2010, causing the interruption of these supportive services for thousands of elderly persons in the city.

23. According to the information in the above passage, funding cuts for the Title V Senior Community Services Employment program would

    A. not affect the availability of home-delivered meals for the elderly
    B. be greater in 2009 because of an overall decline in the city's population

C. result in the loss of 1,484 jobs for the elderly
D. impact mostly on the staff assigned to senior centers

24. Based on the information in the above passage, which of the following statements is MOST correct? 24.____

   A. Funding cuts will affect only a small portion of the city's elderly population.
   B. The largest funding cuts will take place in Title IIIC programs.
   C. The Job Opportunity Program will not be affected by cuts in Title IIIB programs.
   D. Funding for Older Americans Act programs will be cut by an additional 10% in 2010.

25. Based on the information in the above passage, it can be inferred that escort services for the elderly will 25.____

   A. continue in 2009 but be eliminated in 2010
   B. not be affected in 2010 due to prior year funding
   C. be reduced in 2009 and eliminated in 2010
   D. not be affected in 2009 but reduced in 2010

KEY (CORRECT ANSWERS)

1.	C	11.	B
2.	A	12.	A
3.	B	13.	D
4.	C	14.	C
5.	B	15.	C
6.	D	16.	A
7.	A	17.	A
8.	C	18.	B
9.	D	19.	B
10.	C	20.	D

21. A
22. B
23. A
24. C
25. D

EXAMINATION SECTION
TEST 1

DIRECTIONS: Each question or incomplete statement is followed by several suggested answers or completions. Select the one that BEST answers the question or completes the statement. *PRINT THE LETTER OF THE CORRECT ANSWER IN THE SPACE AT THE RIGHT.*

1. You are a Supervisor who is about to evaluate your employees, utilizing the new non-managerial evaluation system.
   Which of the following steps would NOT be useful in achieving optimum objectivity in your evaluations?

   A. Establish mutual performance goals
   B. Focus on actual tasks of the employees
   C. Provide measurable work standards
   D. Assess employees' attitudes and work habits

2. The Child Welfare Reform Act of 1979 was designed to improve and standardize the administration of child welfare services throughout the state.
   One way in which the Human Resources Administration has implemented this Act is by

   A. extending foster care placement until the child's natural family is completely intact
   B. expanding the provision of intensive preventive services to high-risk families
   C. developing a service plan which is focused exclusively on the welfare and needs of the child
   D. reducing the use of day care and homemaker services in case planning

3. In order for a client to be classified as *at risk* in Protective Services for Adults, the client should be

   A. functionally impaired and manifesting disorganized behavior and social disorientation
   B. in danger of becoming psychotic due to inability to cope with major stress
   C. harmed or be threatened by harm which could result in physical or mental injury, neglect, or maltreatment
   D. mentally impaired, resulting in poor memory, orientation, perception, and judgment

4. A subordinate supervisor reports to you that an unknown person is in the office reading a case record.
   As the administrative supervisor, the FIRST action you should take is to

   A. tell the person that case records are confidential
   B. inform the agency director of a possible breach of security
   C. alert building security of an intruder in the office
   D. approach the person and ask for identification

5. A *Section 75* hearing refers to

   A. a step in the appeals process available to a worker who is being brought up on disciplinary charges
   B. a fair hearing where clients ask to have their eligibility reconsidered

C. a step in the grievance procedure open only to managerial employees
D. an unemployment hearing available to a terminated employee who has been rejected for unemployment benefits

6. The area for which you have program responsibility has undergone recent changes. Your staff is now required to perform many new tasks, and morale is low.
The LEAST effective way for you to improve long-term staff morale would be to

   A. develop support groups to discuss problems
   B. involve staff in job development
   C. maintain a comfortable social environment within the group
   D. adequately plan and give assignments in a timely manner

7. There have been some noticeable changes in the behavior of one of your supervisors in an Income Maintenance Unit, and you have evidence that he is taking drugs on a regular basis. However, the usual high quality and quantity of his work to date has declined only slightly. As his supervisor, the BEST course of action for you to take is to

   A. talk to him about the situation and say that you will assist him in getting the help he needs
   B. wait until there is a more noticeable decline in his work performance before talking to him
   C. give him some literature on the dangers of drug addiction
   D. tell him that you want him to make an appointment with the Employee Assistance Unit

8. According to state law, when a person receiving Home Relief or Aid to Dependent Children moves from one social services district in the state to another social services district, also within the state, the client shall

   A. automatically continue to receive public assistance for a period of three months succeeding the move
   B. continue to receive public assistance only if the person continues to be eligible for such assistance
   C. receive public assistance only after filing an application in the new district
   D. continue to receive public assistance from the former district for a period of two months, whether or not the person meets the new district's eligibility requirements

9. The number of homeless persons in the city has increased greatly during the past three years.
Which of the following has contributed LEAST to this increase?

   A. Discharge into the community of state mental hospital patients
   B. Loss of low-priced single room occupancy hotels
   C. Influx of large numbers of illegal aliens
   D. Increased unemployment brought about by the recession

10. As a supervisor in a large office, one of your subordinate supervisors stops you in the middle of the office and complains loudly that he is being treated unfairly. The rest of the staff ceases work and listens to the complaint. The MOST appropriate action for you to take in this situation is to

A. ignore this unprofessional behavior and continue on your way
B. tell the supervisor that his behavior is unprofessional and he should learn how to conduct himself
C. explain to the supervisor why you believe he is not being treated unfairly
D. ask the supervisor to come to your office at a specific time to discuss the matter

11. Although there is no single psychological profile that fits all batterers, men who batter their wives have certain identified psychological characteristics. Which of the following is NOT a psychological characteristic of a batterer?
Batterers

   A. understand the reasons for their frustrations and why they lose control
   B. feel angry a good deal of the time, and their anger escalates rapidly
   C. generally find it difficult to verbally express strong feelings
   D. have a tendency to act before thinking, which often impairs job and social functioning

12. According to a recently legislated change in the statewide Central Register of Child Abuse and Maltreatment, of the following, a prospective foster or adoptive parent who has been the subject of an Indicated Report of Child Abuse or Maltreatment should be

   A. advised by telephone of the reason for denial of application
   B. rejected on the basis of the information in the Register
   C. given a state fair hearing if a request is made to review the report
   D. approved pending evidence of rehabilitation

13. You are a supervisor in a field office where there is a great deal of contact with clients in crisis situations. You have been asked by your director to conduct a training program for newly assigned social services staff who are not experienced in casework intervention in a crisis situation.
The PRIMARY objective of this training program should be to help

   A. motivate the client in crisis to follow through on a plan of action
   B. the caseworker develop skills to help clients restore their sense of stability
   C. the supervisors identify the stages of crisis development
   D. the staff being trained to express their feelings about people in crisis

14. You are told that one of your subordinates is distributing literature which attempts to recruit individuals to join a particular political organization. Several workers complain that their rights are being violated. Of the following, the BEST action for you to take FIRST is to

   A. ignore the situation because no harm is being done
   B. discuss the matter further with your supervisor
   C. ask the worker to stop distributing the literature
   D. tell the workers that they do not have to read the material

15. A former client calls your office stating that he is currently in a mental health program and needs to obtain certain selected personal information from his closed case record.
In this situation, you should tell the client that this information is

   A. *available* only by order of the Supreme Court
   B. *available* under the Freedom of Information Act

C. *not available* unless requested by the mental health agency
D. *not available* because his case is closed

16. As a supervisor in a General Social Services field office, a vendor calls you regarding a Home Care client who has a history of physically and verbally abusing the home attendants assigned to her. The client has had at least 25 home attendants in the past six months, and the vendor now refuses to provide any more.
In this situation, the FIRST action for you to take is to

   A. insist that the vendor fulfill its contractual obligations and continue to provide home attendant services
   B. advise the case manager to discuss the situation with the client so that the reasons for her dissatisfaction with her home attendants can be explored
   C. request a psychiatric evaluation in order to determine whether the client is capable of using the service or should be referred to protective services
   D. discuss the situation with the case manager in order to devise a workable plan for services and treatment

17. Of the following, the use of outside consultants by public welfare agencies has been found to be MOST effective in

   A. analyzing the cost effectiveness of a specific agency program
   B. assessing community service needs and resources
   C. developing and strengthening interagency program planning and relationships
   D. providing technical and professional expertise not otherwise available in the agency

18. Employment and training under the CETA program has been significantly reduced because of recent legislative and administrative changes.
Of the following, it would be MOST correct to conclude that, as a result,

   A. the states will extend unemployment benefits from 26 to 39 weeks
   B. the public assistance caseload will increase, particularly in the Home Relief Program
   C. more stringent work rules will be applied to the Home Relief Program
   D. in a two-parent ADC family, income will be based on that of the principal wage earner during the most recent 24 month period

19. As a supervisor in General Social Services, you are conducting a training course on techniques to be used when interviewing victims of domestic violence, particularly battered women. A caseworker tells you that she has a client whom she suspects is a victim of physical abuse, but she is uncertain as to how to approach the subject with the client. In this situation, you should tell the caseworker that the BEST way to elicit the information is by beginning the next interview with

   A. open-ended indirect questions about the marital relationship
   B. direct questions about the spouse's use of violence in the home
   C. a statement indicating the reasons for suspecting spouse abuse
   D. statistics on domestic violence in the general population

20. As a supervisor, you receive a telephone call from a newspaper reporter who wants information regarding a child welfare case in which, allegedly, appropriate services were not provided.
In this situation, the FIRST action you should take is to

   A. discuss the matter with the reporter in general terms
   B. bring the situation to your supervisor's attention
   C. refer the reporter to the Office of Community Education
   D. transfer the call to the caseworker assigned to the case

21. You have been assigned to develop a short training course for a recently issued procedure.
In designing this course, which of the following statements is the LEAST important for you to consider?

   A. The learning experience must be interesting and meaningful in terms of the staff member's job.
   B. The method of teaching must be strictly followed in order to develop successful learning experiences.
   C. The course content should incorporate the rules and regulations of the agency.
   D. The procedure should be consistent with the agency's objectives.

22. As a supervisor, there are several newly-promoted employees under your supervision. Each of these employees is subject to a probationary period PRIMARILY to

   A. assess the employee's performance to see if the employee should be retained or removed from the position
   B. give the employee the option to return to his former employment if the employee is unhappy in the new position
   C. give the employee an opportunity to learn the duties and responsibilities of the position
   D. judge the employee's potential for upward mobility in the future

23. Which of the following statements MOST accurately describes the clients currently being serviced by HRA's shelters for the homeless?
Over

   A. 75% are women
   B. 75% are alcoholics
   C. 50% are 50 years old or over
   D. 50% are 40 years old or younger

24. Late in the day, a protective services for adults situation is brought to your attention. The caseworker has indicated that a psychiatrist has written an order for placement, but that the client refuses to leave his home. The ambulance staff who were called to the scene refused to take the client to a hospital because there was no evidence of serious illness or injury. The Supervisor I has recommended temporary purchase of Home Care Services. For you, the administrative supervisor, to approve this purchase is APPROPRIATE because the

A. client is *at risk* and services can be provided without regard to income
B. agency staff knows what is best for the client
C. client has refused services and is not seriously ill or injured
D. client may do himself harm and should be placed in an institution

25. A program called PEG (Program to Eliminate the Gap) has been established in an attempt to reduce the impact of decreased federal funding on HRA's ability to continue operation of some social service programs.
Which of the following statements regarding PEG is NOT correct?

   A. Income Maintenance will make a concerted effort to reclassify Public Assistance recipients from the Home Relief Program to federally funded programs.
   B. Special Services for Children will attempt to reduce the cost of children in placement by transferring them to less costly institutional settings.
   C. Family and Adult Services will attempt to move the homeless from shelter care to adult homes and secure SSI for them.
   D. Custodial services will not be contracted out and HRA's own custodial staff will be used for building maintenance.

KEY (CORRECT ANSWERS)

1.	D	11.	A
2.	B	12.	C
3.	C	13.	B
4.	D	14.	C
5.	A	15.	A
6.	C	16.	D
7.	A	17.	D
8.	B	18.	B
9.	C	19.	A
10.	D	20.	C

21. B
22. A
23. D
24. A
25. B

TEST 2

DIRECTIONS: Each question or incomplete statement is followed by several suggested answers or completions. Select the one that BEST answers the question or completes the statement. *PRINT THE LETTER OF THE CORRECT ANSWER IN THE SPACE AT THE RIGHT.*

1. You have been assigned to assume the duties of a recently transferred supervisor in a well established local social services district office. After a while, you learn that your predecessor was extremely well liked, and your staff is blaming you for the transfer.
   The BEST approach for you to take in this situation is to

   A. call a staff meeting in order to explain that you are not responsible for the transfer and want to get along with everyone for the sake of the program
   B. disregard the situation and continue to do your work, hoping that, in time, the resentment toward you will disappear
   C. continue doing your job and, as you hold group meetings, let your staff bring up the issue so it can be openly discussed and resolved
   D. speak to each member of your staff to find out who is blaming you for the transfer in order to identify the source of the problem

   1.____

2. A Supervisor I under your supervision rushes into your office to tell you he has just received a telephone bomb threat.
   As the administrative supervisor, the FIRST thing you should do is

   A. evacuate staff from the floor
   B. call the police and building security
   C. advise your administrator
   D. do a preliminary search

   2.____

3. Assume that you are a supervisor in Family and Adult Services. It is common office knowledge that one of your five unit supervisors has been dating his secretary. Both are married. Recently, they have been screaming at each other in the office. The supervisor has become extremely critical of the secretary's work, and she complains that he is picking on her.
   The MOST appropriate action for you to take is to

   A. meet with both of them to explore whether the three of you can resolve their differences
   B. inform the unit supervisor not to let personal differences with his secretary interfere with his professionalism
   C. tell each of them they should stop dating because their personal relationship is affecting their office work
   D. make staff changes so that the secretary and unit supervisor do not work together

   3.____

4. As a supervisor in the Bureau of Income Support, you suspect that one of your subordinates has been stealing money and valuables from the purses of other employees. The BEST action to take in this situation is to

   A. talk to the staff member whom you suspect and give him an opportunity to respond
   B. tell staff in the surrounding area to watch the suspect carefully and report back to you

   4.____

C. explain the problem to the Special Investigations Unit and ask for their help
D. tell employees not to keep money and valuables in the office

5. As a supervisor in a General Social Services office, you have been designated as conference officer. You have been assigned to resolve a case situation in which the relative of a client is challenging the number of home care hours approved for the client.
In this situation, you should begin the interview with the relative by

   A. sympathizing with him, but state that he will have to go to court if he wants to have the decision changed
   B. explaining exactly how the decision was arrived at, quoting procedures and policy when necessary
   C. telling him that you had nothing to do with the decision and that you will do what you can to get it changed
   D. asking him to tell exactly what he is concerned about and what he proposes as a satisfactory solution

6. Which of the following statements BEST describes Family and Adult Services' Extended Services Program?

   A. A new concept of placing General Social Services Intake staff in an Income Maintenance Center
   B. An attempt to provide defined services to various ethnic groups which make up the community
   C. A program designed to provide shelter for homeless men and women
   D. An extension of a current program which places recent dischargees from mental institutions in family homes

7. Specific tasks and standards have been established by the Human Resources Administration/Department of Social Services for all civil service titles and functional titles used within the agency. In a conference with a subordinate supervisor, you find that the FACTs (Functionally Assigned Cluster of Tasks) for the supervisor's functional title do not correspond with the duties the supervisor performs.
In this situation, the FIRST action you should take is to

   A. arrange for the creation of a new functional title so that the supervisor can be fairly evaluated
   B. bring the supervisor's assigned duties in line with the FACTs established for the functional title
   C. submit the proper forms listing a new set of FACTs selected from the master list
   D. bring the problem to the attention of the local administrator and request a new set of FACTs

8. One of the functions of Family and Adult Services is to provide home attendants for the disabled and elderly in their own homes.
The PRIMARY focus of this service is to

   A. relieve adult children of the responsibility of caring for their parents
   B. provide jobs for a large unskilled section of the population
   C. offer skilled nursing care for the disabled and elderly
   D. keep these clients in the community and avoid institutionalization

9. After reviewing the Absence Control form for a unit under your supervision, you find that one of your staff members has a fifth undocumented sick leave within a six-month period. In this situation, the FIRST action you should take is to

    A. discuss the seriousness of the matter with the staff member when he returns to work and fully document the details of the discussion
    B. review the case with the location director and warn the staff member that future use of sick leave will not be approved
    C. submit the proper disciplinary forms to ensure that the staff member is penalized for excessive absences
    D. request that the timekeeper put the staff member on doctor's note restriction

10. As a supervisor in the Division of Employment, you have just received an anonymous letter alleging that one of your staff members has been taking bribes from a contractor whose program he monitors.
    The MOST appropriate action for you to take is to

    A. call the employee in and confront him with the letter
    B. ask the employee's immediate supervisor to keep a close watch on his activities
    C. refer the letter to the Office of the Inspector General for follow-up
    D. ignore the letter because you feel certain the employee is innocent

11. Title XX of the U.S. Social Security Act provides funding for many of the Human Resources Administration's social services programs.
    Which of the following services provided under Title XX are available only to those income eligible for certain federal or state programs?

    A. Protective Services for Children
    B. Protective Services for Adults
    C. Preventive Services for Children
    D. Preventive Services for Adults

12. You are a supervisor in a placement office in which the telephone is frequently used to contact vendors and clients. One of your subordinates, who does extremely effective work, receives a large number of lengthy personal telephone calls each day. During these calls, there is a distinct lull in the work of the staff in the surrounding area, who listen to the conversation.
    In this situation, you should

    A. tell the worker to sharply reduce the number and length of personal calls received
    B. take no action because the telephone calls do not interfere with the worker's effectiveness
    C. hold a staff meeting and tell subordinates to concentrate on their work and not listen to each other's calls
    D. prepare and distribute a memo to staff limiting personal calls to one a day of two minutes in length

13. In 1982, a statewide pilot program was established which allowed the city to divert a Home Relief recipient's monthly grant to an employer for up to six months in order to encourage private sector job opportunities for welfare clients.
    This project was established as part of the

A. Work Incentive Program (WIN)
B. Comprehensive Employment Training Act (CETA)
C. Adult Work Experience and Training Program (AWET)
D. Temporary Employment Assistance Program (TEAP)

14. As a supervisor in Family and Adult Services, you have been advised that you may select several outstanding employees for merit increases. After submitting the name of an employee who has been performing exceedingly well, and informing him that you have done so, you are told that he is not eligible for a merit increase under the present guidelines because he is earning over the maximum for his title.
The BEST way to handle this situation is to

    A. let the employee think that his name is being submitted
    B. inform the employee that you are working to revise the agency guidelines so that he would be eligible for a merit increase next year
    C. discuss with the employee the possibility of assuming higher level responsibilities so that he can be recommended for a provisional promotion
    D. tell the employee that he will be eligible to receive a merit increase the next fiscal year

15. The Utility Disconnection Program (UDP) was established in 1978 to prevent crises caused by the imminent or actual disconnection of heat-related utilities due to non-payment of bills.
If lack of heat would create a hardship, hazard, or life-threatening situation, the utility company may NOT shut off the heat-related utility

    A. for the time span for which the Department of Social Services will guarantee payment
    B. during the winter heating season, which lasts from November 1st through April 15th
    C. provided that the residents agree to apply for public assistance in order to pay the bills
    D. as long as GSS workers make visits each month to verify that conditions have not changed

16. Of the following, the MOST important consideration in deciding to place a child in a foster home in the geographic vicinity where the natural parent lives is whether the

    A. needed services are available in the community
    B. parent has a history of violence and abuse
    C. child has a history of running away
    D. parent has expressed a desire to surrender the child

17. A subordinate supervisor recently assigned to your office begins his first conference with you by saying that he has learned something that another supervisor is doing that you should know about.
After hearing this statement, of the following, the BEST approach for you to take is to

    A. explain to the supervisor that the conference is to discuss his work and not that of his co-workers
    B. tell the supervisor that you do not encourage a *spy system* among the staff you supervise

C. tell the supervisor that you will listen to his report only if the other supervisor is present
D. allow the supervisor to continue talking until you have enough information to make a decision on how best to respond

18. Assume that you are a supervisor recently assigned to a new unit. You notice that, for the past few days, one of the employees in your unit whose work is about average has been stopping work at about four o'clock and has been spending the rest of the afternoon relaxing at his desk.
The BEST of the following actions for you to take in this situation is to

   A. assign more work to this employee since it is apparent that he does not have enough work to keep him busy
   B. observe the employee's conduct more closely for about ten days before taking any more positive action
   C. discuss the matter with the employee, pointing out to him how he can use the extra hour daily to raise the level of his job performance
   D. question the previous supervisor in charge of the unit in order to determine whether he had sanctioned such conduct when he supervised that unit

19. According to a Social Services law, a judge may terminate parental rights if, after a year of foster care, a fair preponderance of the evidence suggests that the agency's *diligent efforts* have failed to improve the parents' willingness or ability to care for their child.
In a Supreme Court ruling, Santosky v. Kramer, this law was declared unconstitutional because

   A. the term *diligent efforts* should be more clearly defined
   B. a higher standard of proof for permanent neglect situations is required
   C. termination of parental rights is too severe an action to be taken after only a year
   D. the importance of the natural family unit was not sufficiently emphasized

20. You are a supervisor in the Service Section of a local Income Maintenance Center. It has been brought to your attention that one of the field workers in this section has been seen several times clocking out for the field but has gone home instead.
Of the following, the LEAST desirable *initial* action to take is to

   A. review the worker's case records to compare them against the field activity control form
   B. review the worker's personnel folder to review past areas of performance and performance problems
   C. discuss the situation with both the field worker's supervisor and the field worker
   D. call Special Investigations to have the field worker put under surveillance

21. A new supervisor was assigned to your program four months ago. Although he tries hard, he has been unable to meet certain standards because he still has a lot to learn.
As his supervisor, you are required to submit performance evaluations within a few days.
How would you rate this employee on the tasks where he fails to meet standards because of lack of experience?

   A. Satisfactory   B. Conditional
   C. Unsatisfactory   D. Unratable

22. Rumors have arisen to the effect that one of the Social Investigators under your supervision has been attending classes at a local university during afternoon hours when he is supposed to be making field visits.
    The BEST of the following ways for you to approach this problem is to

    A. disregard the rumors since, like most rumors, they probably have no actual foundation in fact
    B. have a discreet investigation made in order to determine the actual facts prior to taking any other action
    C. inform the investigator that you know what he has been doing and that such behavior is overt dereliction of duty and is punishable by dismissal
    D. review the investigator's work record, spot check his cases, and take no further action unless the quality of his work is below average for the unit

23. The City Fair Hearing Review Unit can direct that an income maintenance case be withdrawn from the Fair Hearing Process when

    A. the original notice of intent was improperly prepared by the Liaison and Adjustment Section
    B. the Income Maintenance Center has taken the appropriate steps to withdraw the case
    C. the review of the documentation packet indicates that there is insufficient evidence to support the proposed action
    D. the Liaison and Adjustment Section settles the case before the date of the scheduled Fair Hearing

24. In recent years, human services organizations have adopted modern management tools and techniques originally developed in the business sector in order to increase effectiveness and efficiency in delivering services to clients.
    Which of the following is GENERALLY an important element of this approach to human service organization management?

    A. Considering the socio-political milieu and the influence it exerts over the organization
    B. Developing clearly articulated and workable goals based on valid data, staff participation, and client needs
    C. Originating solutions on the basis of a particular problem, instead of employing solutions already at hand
    D. Using open-ended case management as a basic strategy of programming for caseworkers

25. As the supervisor in a program servicing teenage mothers, you have been asked to train your staff in the utilization of group work techniques with these clients. Your subordinates have been dealing with this population on a one-to-one basis only and feel anxious about facing more than one client at a time.
    Of the following, the LEAST essential topic to be covered in your training session is

    A. differences between working with one person and with a group of people
    B. methods of observing the interaction among group participants
    C. sources of referral for teenage mothers both in the agency and in the community
    D. methods of reviewing and analyzing content of group sessions

KEY(CORRECT ANSWERS)

1.	C	11.	D
2.	B	12.	A
3.	D	13.	D
4.	C	14.	C
5.	D	15.	B
6.	B	16.	A
7.	A	17.	D
8.	D	18.	C
9.	B/A	19.	B
10.	C	20.	D

21. B
22. B
23. C
24. B
25. C

EXAMINATION SECTION
TEST 1

DIRECTIONS: Each question or incomplete statement is followed by several suggested answers or completions. Select the one that BEST answers the question or completes the statement. *PRINT THE LETTER OF THE CORRECT ANSWER IN THE SPACE AT THE RIGHT.*

1. Assume that you are a supervisor. One of the workers under your supervision is careless about the routine aspects of his work.
   Of the following, the action MOST likely to develop in this worker a better attitude toward job routines is to demonstrate that

   A. it is just as easy to do his job the right way
   B. organization of his job will leave more time for field work
   C. the routine part of the job is essential to performing a good piece of work
   D. job routines are a responsibility of the worker

2. A supervisor can MOST effectively secure necessary improvement in a worker's office work by

   A. encouraging the worker to keep abreast of his work
   B. relating the routine part of his job to the total job to be done
   C. helping the worker to establish a good system for covering his office work and holding him to it
   D. informing the worker that he will be required to organize his work more efficiently

3. A supervisor should offer criticism in such a manner that the criticism is helpful and not overwhelming.
   Of the following, the LEAST valid inference that can be drawn on the basis of the above statement is that a supervisor should

   A. demonstrate that the criticism is partial and not total
   B. give criticism in such a way that it does not undermine the worker's self-confidence
   C. keep his relationships with the worker objective
   D. keep criticism directed towards general work performance

4. The one of the following areas in which a worker may LEAST reasonably expect direct assistance from the supervisor is in

   A. building up rapport with all clients
   B. gaining insight into the unmet needs of clients
   C. developing an understanding of community resources
   D. interpreting agency policies and procedures

5. You are informed that a worker under your supervision has submitted a letter complaining of an unfair service rating. Of the following, the MOST valid assumption for you to make concerning this worker is that he should be

   A. more adequately supervised in the future
   B. called in for a supervisory conference
   C. given a transfer to some other unit where he may be more happy
   D. given no more consideration than any other inefficient worker

6. Assume that you are a supervisor. You find that a somewhat bewildered worker, newly appointed to the department, hesitates to ask questions for fear of showing his ignorance and jeopardizing his position.
Of the following, the BEST procedure for you to follow is to

   A. try to discover the reason for his evident fear of authority
   B. tell him that when he is in doubt about a procedure or a policy, he should consult his fellow workers
   C. develop with the worker a plan for more frequent supervisory conferences
   D. explain why each staff member is eager to give him any available information that will help him do a good job

7. Of the following, the MOST effective method of helping a newly appointed worker adjust to his new job is to

   A. assure him that with experience his uncertain attitudes will be replaced by a professional approach
   B. help him, by accepting him as he is, to have confidence in his ability to handle the job
   C. help him to be on guard against the development of punitive attitudes
   D. help him to recognize the mutability of the agency's policies and procedures

8. Suppose that, as a supervisor, you have scheduled an individual conference with an experienced worker under your supervision.
Of the following, the BEST plan of action for this conference is to

   A. discuss the cases that the worker is most interested in
   B. plan with the worker to cover the problems in his cases that are difficult for him
   C. advise the worker that the conference is his to do with as he sees fit
   D. spot check the worker's case load in advance and select those cases for discussion in which the worker has done poor work

9. Of the following, the CHIEF function of a supervisor should be to

   A. assist in the planning of new policies and the evaluation of existing ones
   B. promote congenial relationships among members of the staff
   C. achieve optimum functioning of each unit and each worker
   D. promote the smooth functioning of job routines

10. The competent supervisor must realize the importance of planning.
Of the following, the aspect of planning which is LEAST appropriately considered a responsibility of the supervisor is

    A. long-range planning for the proper functioning of his unit
    B. planning to take care of peak and slack periods
    C. planning to cover agency policies in group conferences
    D. long-range planning to develop community resources

11. The one of the following objectives which should be of LEAST concern to the supervisor in the performance of his duties is to

    A. help the worker to make friends with all of his clients
    B. be impartial and fair to all members of the staff
    C. stimulate the worker's growth on the job
    D. meet the needs of individual workers for case work guidance

12. The one of the following which is LEAST properly considered a direct responsibility of the supervisor is

    A. liaison between the staff and the administrator
    B. interpreting administrative orders and procedures to the worker
    C. training new workers
    D. maintaining staff morale at a high level

13. In order to teach the worker to develop an objective approach, the BEST action for the supervisor to take is to help the worker to

    A. develop a sincere interest in his job
    B. understand the varied responsibilities that are an integral part of his job
    C. differentiate clearly between himself as a friend and as a case worker
    D. find satisfaction in his work

14. If the worker shows excessive submission which indicates a need for dependence on the supervisor in handling a case, it would be MOST advisable for the supervisor to

    A. indicate firmly that the worker-supervisor relationship does not call for submission
    B. define areas of responsibility of worker and of supervisor
    C. recognize the worker's need to be sustained and supported and help him by making decisions for him
    D. encourage the worker to do his best to overcome his handicap

15. Assume that, as a supervisor, you are conducting a group conference.
    Of the following, the BEST procedure for you to follow in order to stimulate group discussion is to

    A. permit the active participation of all members
    B. direct the discussion to an acceptable conclusion
    C. resolve conflicts of opinion among members of the group
    D. present a question for discussion on which the group members have some knowledge or experience

16. Suppose that, as a new supervisor, you wish to inform the staff under your supervision of your methods of operation. Of the following, the BEST procedure for you to follow is to

    A. advise the staff that they will learn gradually from experience
    B. inform each worker in an individual conference
    C. call a group conference for this purpose
    D. distribute a written memorandum among all members of the staff

17. The MOST constructive and effective method of correcting a worker who has made a mistake is, in general, to

    A. explain that his evaluation is related to his errors
    B. point out immediately where he erred and tell him how it should have been done
    C. show him how to readjust his methods so as to avoid similar errors in the future
    D. try to discover by an indirect method why the error was made

18. The MOST effective method for the supervisor to follow in order to obtain the cooperation of a worker under his supervision is, wherever possible, to

    A. maintain a careful record of performance in order to keep the worker on his toes
    B. give the worker recognition in order to promote greater effort and give him more satisfaction in his work
    C. try to gain the worker's cooperation for the good of the welfare service
    D. advise the worker that his advancement on the job depends on his cooperation

19. Of the following, the MOST appropriate initial course for a worker to take when he is unable to clarify a policy with his supervisor is to

    A. bring up the problem at the next group conference
    B. discuss the policy immediately with his fellow workers
    C. accept the supervisor's interpretation as final
    D. determine what responsibility he has for putting the policy into effect

20. Good administration allows for different treatment of different workers.
    Of the following, the CHIEF implication of this statement is that

    A. it would be unfair for the supervisor not to treat all staff members alike
    B. fear of favoritism tends to undermine staff morale
    C. best results are obtained by individualization within the limits of fair treatment
    D. difficult problems call for a different kind of approach

21. The MOST effective and appropriate method of building efficiency and morale in a group of workers is, in general,

    A. by stressing the economic motive
    B. through use of the authority inherent in the position
    C. by a friendly approach to all
    D. by a discipline that is fair but strict

22. Of the following, the LEAST valid basis for the assignment of work to an employee is the

    A. kind of service to be rendered
    B. experience and training of the worker
    C. health and capacity of the worker
    D. racial composition of the community where the office is located

23. The CHIEF justification for staff education, consisting of in-service training, lies in its contribution to   23._____

    A. improvement in the quality of work performed
    B. recruitment of a better type of worker to the department
    C. employee morale, accruing from a feeling of growth on the job
    D. the satisfaction that the worker gets on his job

24. Suppose that you are a supervisor. A worker no longer with the department requests   24._____
you, as his former supervisor, to write a letter recommending him for a position with a private organization.
Of the following, the BEST procedure for you to follow is to include in the letter only information that

    A. will help the applicant get the job
    B. is clear, factual, and substantiated
    C. is known to you personally
    D. can readily be corroborated by personal interview

25. Of the following, the MOST important item on which to base the efficiency evaluation of a   25._____
worker under your supervision is

    A. the nature of the relationship that he has built up with his clients
    B. how he gets along with his fellow employees
    C. his personal habits and skills
    D. the effectiveness of his control over his case load

KEY (CORRECT ANSWERS)

1.	D	11.	A
2.	B	12.	A
3.	D	13.	C
4.	A	14.	B
5.	B	15.	D
6.	C	16.	C
7.	B	17.	C
8.	B	18.	B
9.	C	19.	D
10.	D	20.	C

21. D
22. D
23. A
24. B
25. D

TEST 2

DIRECTIONS: Each question or incomplete statement is followed by several suggested answers or completions. Select the one that BEST answers the question or completes the statement. *PRINT THE LETTER OF THE CORRECT ANSWER IN THE SPACE AT THE RIGHT*

1. According to generally accepted personnel practice, the MOST effective method of building morale in a new worker is to   1.____

    A. exercise caution in praising the worker, lest he become overconfident
    B. give sincere and frank commendation whenever possible in order to stimulate interest and effort
    C. praise the worker highly even for mediocre performance so that he will be stimulated to do better
    D. warn the worker frequently that he cannot hope to succeed unless he puts forth his best effort

2. Errors made by newly appointed workers often follow a predictable pattern.   2.____
The one of the following errors likely to have LEAST serious consequences is the tendency of a new worker to

    A. discuss problems that are outside his province with the client
    B. persuade the client to accept the worker's solution of a problem
    C. be too strict in carrying out departmental policy and procedure
    D. depend upon the use of authority due to his inexperience and lack of skill in working with people

3. Of the following, the BEST method of helping the new worker to apply social case work principles is, in general, through   3.____

    A. the medium of the individual conference
    B. reading generally accepted authorities on the subject
    C. the medium of his own cases
    D. a course of study for him to follow

4. The MOST effective way for a supervisor to break down a worker's defensive stand against supervisory guidance is to   4.____

    A. come to an understanding with him on the mutual responsibilities involved in the job of the worker and supervisor
    B. tell him he must feel free to express his opinions and to discuss basic problems
    C. show him how to develop toward greater objectivity, sensitivity, and understanding
    D. advise him that it is necessary to carry out agency policy and procedures in order to do a good job

5. Of the following, the LEAST essential function of the supervisor who is conducting a group conference should be to   5.____

    A. keep attention focused on the purpose of the conference
    B. encourage discussion of controversial points
    C. make certain that all possible viewpoints are discussed
    D. be thoroughly prepared in advance

6. When conducting a group conference, the supervisor should be LEAST concerned with

   A. providing an opportunity for the free interchange of ideas
   B. imparting knowledge and understanding of case work
   C. leading the discussion toward a planned goal
   D. pointing out where individual workers have erred in case work practice

7. If the participants in a conference are unable to agree on the proper application of a concept to the work of the department, the MOST suitable temporary procedure for the supervisor to follow is to

   A. suggest that each member think the subject through before the next meeting
   B. tell the group to examine their differences for possible conflicts with present policies
   C. suggest that practices can be changed because of new conditions
   D. state the acceptable practice in the agency and whether deviations from such practice can be permitted

8. If a worker is to participate constructively in any group discussion, it is MOST important that he have

   A. advance notice of the agenda for the meeting
   B. long experience in the department
   C. knowledge and experience in social work
   D. the ability to assume a leadership role

9. Of the following, the MOST important principle for the supervisor to follow when conducting a group discussion is that he should

   A. move the discussion toward acceptance by the group of a particular point of view
   B. express his ideas clearly and succinctly
   C. lead the group to accept the authority inherent in his position
   D. contribute to the discussion from his knowledge and experience

10. The one of the following which is considered LEAST important as a purpose of the group conference is to

    A. provide for a free exchange of ideas among the members of the group
    B. evaluate case work methods and procedures in order to protect the members from individual criticism
    C. provide an opportunity to interpret procedures and general case work practices
    D. pool the experience of the group members for the benefit of all

11. In order for the evaluation conference to stimulate MOST effectively the worker's professional growth on the job, it should

    A. start him thinking about his present status with the agency
    B. show him the necessity for taking stock of his total performance
    C. give him a sense of direction in relation to his future development
    D. give him a better perspective on the work of the department

12. The PRIMARY consideration in good case recording is that the case history should

    A. be written simply and contain only significant and relevant material
    B. contain subjective material needed on the case
    C. be written concisely and clearly in good English
    D. include points of interest to both the worker and the supervisor

13. Of the following, the MOST important purpose of the case record summary in the department of welfare is to

    A. acquaint the worker with forgotten details of the case
    B. provide a review of the client's status and eligibility
    C. provide a detailed picture of what has happened in the case
    D. give the worker a new perspective on the case

14. The development of good public relations in the area for which the supervisor is responsible should be considered by the supervisor as

    A. not his responsibility as he is primarily responsible for his workers' services
    B. dependent upon him as he is in the best position to interpret the department to the community
    C. not important to the adequate functioning of the department
    D. a part of his method of carrying out his job responsibility as what his workers do affect the community

15. Assume that you are a supervisor. A newly appointed worker under your supervision asks you what action he should take when, finding it necessary to refuse relief to a client, the client becomes unusually belligerent and refuses to listen to reason.
    Of the following, the BEST advice for you to give the worker is to

    A. refer the client to the case supervisor
    B. explain to the client at length the reasons for the refusal
    C. carefully explore with the client all possible courses of action
    D. be firm and definite in his refusal

16. Of the following, the LEAST accurate statement concerning the relationship of public and private social agencies is that

    A. both have an important and necessary function to perform
    B. they are not to be considered as competing or rival agencies
    C. they are cooperating agencies
    D. their work is based on fundamentally different social work concepts

17. Of the following, the LEAST accurate statement concerning the worker-client relationship is that the worker should have the ability to

    A. express warmth of feeling in appropriate ways as a basis for a professional relationship which creates confidence
    B. feel appropriately in the relationship without losing the ability to see the situation in the perspective necessary to help the people immersed in it
    C. identify himself with the client so that the worker's personality does not influence the client
    D. use keen observation and perceive what is significant with a new range of appreciation of the meaning of the situation to the client

18. Of the following, the MOST fundamental psychological concept underlying case work in the public assistance field is that

    A. eligibility for public assistance should be reviewed from time to time
    B. workers should be aware of the prevalence of psychological disabilities among members of families on public assistance
    C. workers should realize the necessity of carrying out the policies laid down by the state office in order that state aid may be received
    D. in the process of receiving assistance, recipients should not be deprived of their normal status of self-direction

19. Of the following, the MOST comprehensive, as well as the MOST accurate, statement concerning the professional attitude of the social worker is that he should

    A. have a real concern for, and an intelligent interest in, the welfare of the client
    B. recognize that the client's feelings rather than the realities of his needs are of major importance to the client
    C. put at the client's service the worker's knowledge and sincere interest in him
    D. use his insight and understanding to make sound decisions about the client

20. The one of the following reasons for refusing a job which is LEAST acceptable, from the viewpoint of maintaining a client's continued rights to unemployment insurance benefits, is that

    A. acceptance of the job would interfere with the client's joining or retaining membership in a labor union
    B. there is a strike, lockout, or other industrial controversy in the establishment where employment is offered
    C. the distance from the place of employment to his home is greater than seems justified to the client
    D. the wages offered are lower than the prevailing wages in that locality

21. The one of the following statements concerning the division of veterans assistance which is LEAST accurate is that the service includes

    A. the arrangement of occupational registration, vocational rehabilitation, and employment referrals for veterans and their dependents
    B. aid in obtaining citizenship papers under special naturalization, laws applicable only to veterans
    C. the handling of claims for burial expenses of deceased honorably discharged veterans
    D. providing for hospital care and domiciliary care at soldiers' homes

22. Whenever possible, a client on home relief who is eligible for assistance under one of the three categories should be changed to categorical relief.
   Of the following, the LEAST accurate statement regarding this change is that

   A. change to categorical relief increases public understanding of the purposes and functioning of relief
   B. change to categorical relief is in accordance with the plan of the state department of welfare
   C. the Federal government reimburses the state and city for a percentage under the categories
   D. the welfare client will be better served under one of the forms of categorical relief

23. The LEAST accurate of the following statements regarding the functions of the transportation unit of the department of welfare is that it

   A. provides transportation for persons who have verified offers of employment in states which border on New York State
   B. determines eligibility for payment of transportation expenses
   C. makes reservations and purchases tickets for blind clients who are leaving for temporary periods
   D. is authorized to furnish transportation to all those who meet requirements regardless of whether or not they are in receipt of public assistance

24. The PRIMARY purpose of the welfare department will be BEST fulfilled, insofar as the giving of public assistance is concerned, if the rules and regulations are interpreted

   A. to the end that the most economical operation of the department will result
   B. strictly according to written instructions
   C. with special consideration for those applicants having the greatest needs
   D. insofar as possible in line with each applicant's circumstances and needs

25. The National Mental Health Act provides for

   A. an appropriation of five million dollars for research on mental illness
   B. the organization of a National Mental Health Institution within the structure of the Public Health Service
   C. an appropriation of five million dollars for grants-in-aid to the states for research and expansion of training and clinical facilities
   D. the establishment of Mental Hygiene Clinics in certain specified areas

KEY (CORRECT ANSWERS)

1. B	6. D	11. C	16. D	21. D
2. C	7. D	12. A	17. C	22. D
3. C	8. A	13. B	18. D	23. A
4. A	9. D	14. D	19. C	24. D
5. B	10. B	15. D	20. C	25. B

EXAMINATION SECTION
TEST 1

DIRECTIONS: Each question or incomplete statement is followed by several suggested answers or completions. Select the one the BEST answers the question or completes the statement. *PRINT THE LETTER OF THE CORRECT ANSWER IN THE SPACE AT THE RIGHT.*

1. During an assessment interview, a social worker and a client try to clarify and analyze the client's sense of self. If the worker wants to discover something about the client's spirituality, which of the following questions is MOST appropriate?

    A. Do you have regrets or guilt about the past?
    B. How do you explain or make sense out of the suffering and pain you and others experience in life?
    C. How do you want to be remembered after you die?
    D. Are you comfortable with your membership in your family?

    1.____

2. In general, Americans with strong Asian cultural traditions are LEAST likely to be receptive to _____ support services.

    A. psychological
    B. financial
    C. educational
    D. material

    2.____

3. A client comes to a social worker with multiple problems related to his poor health, unemployment, and low income. In developing an intervention plan, the social worker should FIRST

    A. have the client identify and list what he sees as problems or concerns
    B. have the client identify the significant others who are affected by the problems
    C. offer recommendations for what problems need to be addressed
    D. identify the two or three most significant problems that need to be addressed

    3.____

4. A social history report includes the statement "X completed three years at the University of Kansas and then transferred to Stanford University, where he is currently a senior in education." This should be included under the heading

    A. Family Background and Situation
    B. Use of Community Resources
    C. Intellectual Functioning
    D. Such a statement shouldn't appear at all in a social history report

    4.____

5. When a social system adapts to environmental conditions, _____ has occurred.

    A. Assimilation
    B. Accommodation
    C. Acculturation
    D. Adaptation

    5.____

6. Of the statements below, which BEST states the purpose of staff development in a social services agency?

    6.____

A. advance one's career through study
B. improve performance through enhanced skills
C. acquire and apply new knowledge
D. orient oneself to an organization

7. The primary criticism leveled against the use of self-anchored scales for practice evaluation is mat they

   A. focus on the practitioner rather than the client
   B. do not measure internal states
   C. require training in order to implement
   D. are too subjective

8. Classification skills that emerge in middle childhood involve a mental ability known as

   A. object permanence
   B. decentering
   C. scripting
   D. detachment

9. "Mezzo" social work practice refers to practice with

   A. groups
   B. families
   C. communities
   D. an individual

10. When considering who is a member of a family system, the _____ is the point that divides those who are continually interacting around family concerns and those who have little or no input into family functioning.

    A. boundary
    B. period
    C. margin
    D. focal system

11. The functions of coping mechanisms include
    I. protecting an individual against anxiety
    II. solving problems
    III. reducing the emotional discomfort caused by stressors

    A. I and II
    B. I and III
    C. II and III
    D. I, II and III

12. The most universally held perspective among social workers is the _____ perspective.

    A. ecosystems
    B. generalist
    C. task-centered
    D. psychodynamic

13. Adult protective service programs supported by state statutes protect elderly people from abuse and neglect under the doctrine of

    A. parens patriae
    B. habeas corpus
    C. in loco parentis
    D. volenti non fit iniuria

14. Which of the following generally does the LEAST to contribute to an adolescent's process of individuation?

    A. Maintaining consistent peer relations
    B. Achieving a sexual identity
    C. Working a part-time job
    D. Completing a high-school education

15. During an interview with a client, the client's response to a practitioner's statement suggests that the client has heard exactly the opposite of what was said. This is an example of

    A. projection
    B. reaction formation
    C. displacement
    D. repression

16. During an interview, a client expresses feelings of being different or deviant Which of the following techniques would be MOST appropriate for counteracting these feelings?

    A. Encouragement
    B. Reassurance
    C. Negative reinforcement
    D. Universalization

17. Which of the following statements about suicide is FALSE?

    A. Suicide occurs most frequently as a result of severe depression.
    B. People who talk about suicide rarely follow through with the act
    C. Among adolescents, boys are more likely to succeed in a suicide attempt than girls
    D. People commit suicide at almost every stage of the life cycle.

18. Which of the following elements can be drawn into a one-page ecomap?
    I. Informal resources and natural helpers
    II. Social activities and interests
    III. Job situation, employment, and responsibilities
    IV. Age, sex, and marital status

    A. I and IV
    B. I, II, and IV
    C. IV only
    D. I, II, III, and IV

19. In order to be functional and appropriate for the situation, a professional social worker/client relationship must

A. be established in the initial stages by the worker's statement of purpose
B. be determined by the client's willingness to accept the worker's intervention
C. establish itself early, with an empathetic response to a client's statement of need
D. develop from the worker's joint problem-solving work with clients

20. Which of the following assessment instruments is used to graphically depict barriers and supports that affect a person's interactions with his or her social environment?

    A. Life cycle matrix
    B. Social network grid
    C. The dual perspective
    D. Self-anchored rating scale

21. The phenomenon of "groupthink" is promoted by a number of factors. Which of the following is NOT typically one of them?

    A. Members have an illusion of vulnerability that compels them to avoid risk.
    B. Members have an unquestioning belief in the group's moral lightness.
    C. Social measures of disapproval are applied to dissenters.
    D. Members keep quiet about misgivings and internally minimize their importance.

22. Which of me following is NOT an advantage associated with the use of written service contracts?

    A. Definitive legal status
    B. Clarity of purpose
    C. Unalterable reference point
    D. Reduced client-worker conflict

23. Which of the following is NOT typically involved in the intervention technique known as behavioral rehearsal?

    A. The worker makes suggestions for how to more effectively handle a situation.
    B. The client assumes the role of himself/herself in a role play.
    C. The worker identifies the client's appropriate behaviors after the role-play.
    D. The client describes how he or she would act in a certain situation.

24. Which of the following statements is/are TRUE?
    I. Most elderly people are residents of nursing homes
    II. There are generally more elderly women than men in the population
    III. The elderly are increasing, in numbers as well as a percentage of the population
    IV. Most elderly people move many times following retirement

    A. I only
    B. II and III
    C. III and IV
    D. I, II, III and IV

25. The most important consideration for a worker who looks to collateral information sources during a social work assessment is

    A. the possible hidden agendas of collateral sources
    B. the limited time in which most workers have to gather assessment data

C. whether the collateral sources of information genuinely want to help change the situation
D. whether the client has signed appropriate release forms

26. Which of the following approaches to social work presumes that a client will be involuntary?

    A. Reality therapy
    B. Structural
    C. Behavioral
    D. Psychodynamic

27. A social worker's "duty to warn" presents a potential conflict with the ethical principle of

    A. cultural sensitivity
    B. self-determination
    C. competence
    D. confidentiality

28. During an assessment interview, a client describes her relationship with her husband as a strong positive influence. In putting together an ecomap of this client and her environment, the social worker would depict this relationship by using

    A. a line with several vertical hashmarks (-I-I-I-I-I-I-)
    B. an arrow pointing away from the husband, toward the client
    C. a dotted line
    D. a heavy black line

29. Typically, the _____ stage of an interview is the one which is most powerful in determining the interviewee's impression of the interview as a whole.

    A. opening
    B. questioning
    C. closing
    D. discussion

30. During a client assessment, each of the following should be considered a useful question, EXCEPT

    A. Who do you think bears most of the responsibility for the current problem?
    B. Despite your current problems, what parts of your life are going fairly well?
    C. What would you not change about yourself or your life?
    D. Where did you find the energy to deal with problems like this in the past?

31. A social worker's best defense against a malpractice suit or complaint is usually

    A. a vigorous legal advocate
    B. the testimony of professional character witnesses
    C. a counterclaim against the plaintiff
    D. detailed case records

32. For social service professionals who are responsible for making decisions about the type of program or service that would be most appropriate for a particular client, the most useful assessment instrument is probably a(n)

A. social history
B. collateral data set
C. genogram
D. ecomap

33. During an interview with a family, a practitioner observes that the youngest son often exhibits overly adaptive behavior—he strenuously attempts to comfort the father when the father appears to be upset. Later, the practitioner learns that in school, the child often becomes uneasy or upset whenever another child cries or acts out. The practitioner should interpret these signs as suggestive of possible

A. repressed memories of past trauma
B. sexual abuse
C. formation of a dysfunctional triad
D. physical abuse

34. The primary purpose of a Gantt chart in agency planning is to provide a visual depiction of the relationship between

A. the resources demanded by a project and the resources that are readily available
B. the possible alternatives in a plan and their likely corresponding outcomes
C. the activities required by a project and the time frame for completion
D. the people within an agency and their specific functions

35. A social worker sits down to assess a child who is currently struggling with behavior problems at school. Which of the following assessment instruments should be considered by the worker as especially useful in shedding light on the current situation?

A. Life history grid
B. Self-anchored rating scale
C. Social network map
D. Genogram

36. Which of the following is NOT an advantage associated with the use of multiworker family assessments?

A. Creation of several consultants who may be helpful to the primary worker
B. Firmer post-assessment commitment on the part of family members
C. More open discussion of issues
D. Considerably shorter data-gathering stage

37. The idea that a social system not only adapts to an environment, but in turn has a direct influence on the environment through feedback cycles, is an element of the theory of

A. chaos
B. coevolution
C. synergy
D. autopoiesis

38. Forcing the mentally disabled to work without pay is a violation of the _____ Amendment to the Constitution.

A. Fourth
B. Ninth

C. Thirteenth
D. Sixteenth

39. School-age children are involved in mastering the skills of the _____ stage of cognitive development

    A. preoperational thought
    B. formal operations
    C. sensorimotor
    D. concrete operations

40. Which of the following communication variables is a cognitive barrier to effective transmission?

    A. Speech impediment
    B. Distractions
    C. Language competence
    D. Speech inappropriate to context and client jargon

41. Which of the following reinforcement schedules is almost always used in the beginning stages of an intervention program, because of the speed with which behaviors are learned?

    A. Random
    B. Intermittent
    C. Differential
    D. Continuous

42. A client who is a schoolteacher confesses that he is not comfortable in that role, because it requires intellectual and organizational skills that he does not possess. This is an example of

    A. inter-role conflict
    B. role incapacity
    C. role ambiguity
    D. self-role incongruence

43. Which of the following is NOT an example of a social worker fulfilling the operational purpose of a professional relationship?

    A. Lobbying for local tax reforms that will ease the burden on clients
    B. Conducting a behavioral intervention for a child with school behavior problems
    C. Referring a couple to a marriage counselor
    D. Enrolling a young mother in the federal WIC program

44. A client is having trouble managing problems caused by insufficient resources: she's experiencing difficulties in finding employment, hi finding care for her child while she looks for work, and in finding transportation to accomplish simple errands. Which of the following models of social Work would probably be MOST useful for this client?

    A. Crisis intervention
    B. Task-centered
    C. Cognitive-behavioral
    D. Structural

45. A mother's 6-year-old son is not feeling well, so the mother takes him to the local health clinic, where's she's told the boy needs to be admitted to the hospital immediately for extensive testing. The mother wants to stay with the boy, but the administrative nurse refuses her request The mother comes to a practitioner for help. The MOST appropriate first action would be to

   A. check on the child to see if he is okay
   B. tell the mother not to worry and mat the child will be looked after
   C. find out whether the hospital allows parents to stay with their children
   D. tell the mother not to worry and call the administrative nurse to complain about the situation

45.____

46. In a family, rules and social roles are examples of _____, a factor that characterizes the family as a social system.

   A. interdependence
   B. hierarchy
   C. genography
   D. patterns

46.____

47. Which of the following is an advantage associated with the use of professional organizations for providing staff with continuing education?

   A. Identification with practice value
   B. Low costs
   C. Agency control over content
   D. Accountability for performance

47.____

48. Which of the following approaches to family therapy recognizes the tendency of a family to repeat patterns established in prior generations?

   A. Family systems
   B. Structural
   C. Strategic
   D. Social learning

48.____

49. Which of the following statements about the single-system evaluation approach is FALSE?

   A. It makes use of an experimental control groups
   B. Clients or systems are observed repeatedly before, during, and after interventions.
   C. Changes in the outcome measure are noted that coincide with the intervention
   D. It is compatible with clinical practice.

49.____

50. Which of the following ego defense mechanisms is most common among physically ill persons who are experiencing much fear or pain?

   A. Displacement
   B. Reaction formation
   C. Fantasy
   D. Regression

50.____

KEY (CORRECT ANSWERS)

1. B	11. C	21. A	31. D	41. D
2. A	12. B	22. A	32. A	42. D
3. A	13. A	23. B	33. D	43. A
4. C	14. D	24. B	34. C	44. B
5. B	15. B	25. D	35. A	45. C
6. C	16. D	26. A	36. D	46. D
7. D	17. B	27. D	37. B	47. A
8. B	18. D	28. D	38. C	48. A
9. B	19. D	29. C	39. D	49. A
10. A	20. C	30. A	40. C	50. D

TEST 2

DIRECTIONS: Each question or incomplete statement is followed by several suggested answers or completions. Select the one the BEST answers the question or completes the statement. *PRINT THE LETTER OF THE CORRECT ANSWER IN THE SPACE AT THE RIGHT.*

1. A social worker who wants to use a small group as a resource for clients should keep in mind that for preadolescents, a group numbering _____ is preferred.

    A. 3 or 4
    B. 6 to 10
    C. 10 to 12
    D. 12 to 15

2. Significant disadvantages and risks involved in the teamwork approach to solving problems include each of the following, EXCEPT

    A. escalations in cost
    B. greater risk of confidentiality breach
    C. tendency for activities to center on needs of professionals rather than clients
    D. frequent exclusion of clients from meetings

3. What is the term used in systems theory to denote the unique character of a group, analogous to a person's "personality"?

    A. Morphostasis
    B. Syntropy
    C. Schema
    D. Syntality

4. In terms of societal stigma, another term for "self-fulfilling prophecy" is

    A. passing
    B. subculture development
    C. secondary deviance
    D. social rejection

5. A worker assigned to a ward for the criminally insane makes an effort to understand each individual patient's situation. Which of the following professional values or ethics is the worker implementing?

    A. Self-determination
    B. Privacy
    C. Dignity and respect
    D. Competence

6. The "problem search" method is useful for initial interviews with clients who
    I. have more than one problem that needs to be addressed
    II. have requested an agency service that shows a poor understanding of the problem
    III. are involuntary, referred by an agency or family

    A. I only

B. I and II
C. II and III
D. I, II and III

7. Which of the following is a term for a social system's efficient use of energy, as well as the addition of energy to the system from outside?

    A. Entropy
    B. Dynamism
    C. Negative entropy
    D. Synergy

8. In the ecosystems model for analyzing psychosocial factors that impact special populations, a worker first evaluates a client on Level I, the individual level, and eventually expands the analysis to Level V, the _____ level.

    A. Historical
    B. Family
    C. Cultural
    D. Environmental-structural

9. For inmates of the criminal justice system, the right to freedom from cruel and unusual punishment includes
    I. the right to be free from physical abuse and punishment
    II. the right to reasonable opportunity for physical exercise
    III. the right to receive education and training
    IV. the right to adequate medical treatment

    A. I and II
    B. I and III
    C. I, II and IV
    D. I, II, III and IV

10. During a home interview with a single mother, the mother responds to her three-year-old child's repeated interruptions in a harsh and angry manner. Finally, the child is scolded and sent to her room, crying loudly. In this situation, the MOST appropriate response on the part of the practitioner would be to

    A. say, "It must be tough to be both a father and a mother to your child."
    B. say, "I wonder if you might have handled that differently."
    C. say, "I hate to see children cry like that"
    D. ignore the mother's behavior entirely and continue with the interview

11. According to Parsons, there are four functions necessary to a system. Which of the following is NOT one of these?

    A. Differentiation
    B. Goal-directed activity
    C. Pattern maintenance
    D. Adaptation

12. Which of the following is an example of an assessment interview?

A. A vocational rehabilitation counselor interviews a client with a developmental disability to determine grant eligibility.
B. A social worker at a mental hospital seeks background information to understand the problems and social functioning of a patient
C. A worker at a nursing home compiles a social history on a new resident to obtain information on current social and personal problems.
D. A couple having marital problems is counseled on how to handle their troubles.

13. Many social workers operate under the belief that members of an oppressed group have a more immediate, subtle, and critical knowledge of their oppression than do members of the dominant culture. This is a concept known as

    A. implicit stereotyping
    B. cultural relativism
    C. teleology
    D. epistemic privilege

14. The contemporary model of the diagnostic approach to social work is usually referred to as the _____ approach.

    A. ecological
    B. milieu
    C. psychosocial
    D. medical

15. A program evaluation that focuses on the process of social work programs is described as

    A. functional
    B. systemic
    C. transactional
    D. formative

16. Piaget believes school-age children learn to master _____ at this stage of the life span.

    A. object relations
    B. irreversibility
    C. object permanence
    D. conservation

17. In formulating an intervention plan, a social worker writes the following objective: "Mrs. Talley is to obtain counseling for her grief." The MAIN problem with this objective is that it

    A. is too negative
    B. describes an input but ignores the outcome
    C. doesn't name the counselor
    D. doesn't specify when Mrs. Talley will obtain counseling

18. Which of the following principles is used by social workers to guard against abuses of power?

    A. Cultural relativism
    B. Least restrictive environment
    C. Professional competence

D. Advocacy for social justice

19. When cross-cultural social work, it is best for the worker to operate under the assumption that

    A. human personality can generally be reduced to cultural identity
    B. applicants should always interact with a worker from the same culture
    C. cultures are not homogeneous
    D. there are no cross-cultural absolutes

20. Which of the following kinds of authority is/are appropriate in a professional helping relationship?
    I. The authority of social sanction
    II. The authority of power
    III. The authority of knowledge

    A. I only
    B. I and III
    C. II and III
    D. I, II and III

21. As an advocacy technique, pressuring differs from persuasion in that it involves

    A. the invocation of legal remedies
    B. an appeal to reason
    C. forceful action
    D. understanding the opposing viewpoint

22. The developmental task of symbolic thought is most likely to be acquired by an individual between the ages of

    A. 2-4
    B. 5-7
    C. 8-12
    D. 13-17

23. The use of "soft" criteria (such as cooperativeness, adaptability, and attitude) in supervisory social work evaluations

    A. is an unfair use of unverifiable standards and should be avoided
    B. can make an evaluation sterile and of little value if overused
    C. are too difficult to articulate verbally and should be scaled in some quantifiable way in order to avoid accusations of bias or litigation
    D. should be used in conjunction with objective criteria to provide the "big picture" of how a social worker contributes to the agency or organization

24. Which of the following role problems is most likely to occur in times of rapid social change?

    A. Role ambiguity
    B. Role overload
    C. Self-role incongruence
    D. Role rejection

25. Which of the following types of social work practice would typically place the LEAST amount of emphasis on the client's social and environmental factors? 25.____

   A. Structural
   B. Generalist
   C. Psychodynamic
   D. Cognitive-behavioral

KEY (CORRECT ANSWERS)

1. A
2. B
3. D
4. C
5. C

6. C
7. C
8. A
9. A
10. A

11. A
12. A
13. D
14. C
15. D

16. D
17. B
18. B
19. C
20. B

21. C
22. A
23. D
24. A
25. C

TEST 3

DIRECTIONS: Each question or incomplete statement is followed by several suggested answers or completions. Select the one the BEST answers the question or completes the statement. *PRINT THE LETTER OF THE CORRECT ANSWER IN THE SPACE AT THE RIGHT.*

1. Which of the following is an example of a task-focused coping strategy? 1.____

   A. Seeking support
   B. Modeling behaviors after those of others
   C. Talking about an experience
   D. Withholding an emotional investment in a desired by unlikely outcome

2. During an assessment interview, a social worker and a client try to analyze problems hi the client's role performance. The worker is interested in discovering whether the problem is caused by the client's rejection of or lack of interest in the role. Which of the following questions is MOST appropriate to ask the client? 2.____

   A. Do you think you can learn the behaviors needed to perform this role?
   B. Have you ever been punished in any way for the performance of this role?
   C. What do think will happen if there is no change in performance?
   D. Why don't you like performing this role?

3. A social worker visits a family of five who admit to having multiple problems, many of them resulting from the recent death of a grandmother who had much power and control over the household. During the interview, each family members lists his or her problems and concerns, and then the social worker mentions two possible problems that were not mentioned on any family member's list The MOST appropriate next step during mis meeting would be for 3.____

   A. the worker to name the two or three problems of highest priority
   B. the family members to discuss in turn how they feel about the grandmother's death
   C. the family members to examine the list and vote on the two or three problems of highest priority
   D. the family members and worker to review and sort the problems into logical groupings

4. The greater level of physical activity among school-age children, as compared with preschoolers, is attributed to 4.____

   A. changes in perceptual skills
   B. increased brain development
   C. increased muscle development
   D. improved social skills

5. The purpose of metacommunication is to 5.____

   A. identify the objectives of an interview
   B. establish an environment in which barriers to communication are removed
   C. provide whatever symbolic elements are necessary for encoding or decoding the content of a message

D. provide the frame of reference within which a message's content may be interpreted

6. In the parent-child relationship, the parent is expected to provide the child with food, shelter, supervision, and guidance. This is a description of a parent's

   A. role conception
   B. role ambiguity
   C. social role
   D. role overload

7. As a profession, social work addresses the controversial issue of abortion as

   A. an issue which a social worker may refuse to discuss, based on his or her beliefs, but not without a referral to another professional willing to engage in such a discussion
   B. a legal right of every client that must sublimate personal beliefs
   C. an immoral act that must be passively discouraged by social service professionals
   D. an unfortunate by-product of a societal worldview that devalues its most powerless members

8. Which of the following behavioral techniques is/are used to increase the frequency, intensity, or duration of a target behavior?
   I. Positive reinforcement
   II. Negative reinforcement
   III. Extinction
   IV. Punishment

   A. I only
   B. I and II
   C. II and III
   D. II, III and IV

9. The psychodynamic approach to social work is useful for clients who are

   A. heavily burdened by socioeconomic problems
   B. nonverbal
   C. chemically dependent
   D. actively working for change

10. A client's mental illness or drag addiction are most likely to contribute to a problem of role

    A. misconception
    B. incapacity
    C. rejection
    D. ambiguity

11. The percentage of a community's residents over the age of 65 and under 18 is an expression of the community's

    A. dependency ratio
    B. age margin
    C. generational inversion
    D. generic demand for services

12. A client with a poor employment record confesses her anxiety about a coming job interview to a social worker. The client is nervous about the interview because of her lack of experience in such settings, and doesn't really feel as if she knows how to conduct herself properly. The MOST appropriate intervention technique the social worker can use is

    A. behavioral rehearsal
    B. self-esteem building
    C. role reversal
    D. behavioral contracting

13. For a social worker, the process of assessment ends when

    A. the last assessment interview or form has been recorded
    B. a treatment plan has been formulated
    C. the first set of behavioral and/or environmental goals are met
    D. the terminal phase of service is completed

14. Which of the following is an example of a social worker fulfilling the normative purpose of a professional relationship?

    A. Teaching parenting skills to a young mother
    B. Advocating on behalf of a client to avoid an eviction
    C. Lobbying for an increase in child-care benefits to unemployed mothers seeking work
    D. Referring a client family to a family therapist

15. Which of the following is a type of cognitive intervention?

    A. Managing self-talk
    B. Behavioral contracting
    C. Building self-esteem
    D. Role reversal

16. In response to a high number gay and lesbian runaways on the streets of a community, the director of a social services agency called together a group of prominent lesbian and gay community leaders who would help to define a solution, and to make initial contacts to confirm interest In this way, the director sought

    A. professional consultation
    B. to assess the community
    C. to legitimize the problem
    D. a redefinition of the problem

17. Time-series data are often characterized by their central tendency or location. Another term for this characteristic is

    A. level
    B. validity
    C. trend
    D. variability

18. During an interview with a father and his young daughter, the practitioner picks up signs that the father is invested to an unusual degree in whether the daughter makes the school basketball team hi the coming week of tryouts. On several occasions, the father has mentioned the daughter's past achievements with pride-but the daughter seems slightly embarrassed by his interest. During the remainder of the assessment, the practitioner should spend at least some time exploring the possibility that the relationship between these two is

    A. disengaged
    B. incestuous
    C. enmeshed
    D. closed

19. Most appropriately, a committee of co-workers at a social service agency should perform the hiring function(s) of
    I. screening applicants
    II. recommending a "short list" to hiring personnel
    III. assisting with employment interviews
    IV. voting on final hiring decisions

    A. I and II
    B. II and III
    C. II, III and IV
    D. I, II, III and IV

20. Which of the following statements about a triadic process is TRUE?

    A. It is usually characterized by inappropriate generational boundaries
    B. It refers to the formation of a three-person subsystem
    C. It is often socioeconomic in origin
    D. It introduces cultural features into the arena of boundary management

21. Which of the following statements is FALSE?

    A. Homeless people have federally guaranteed "squatters' rights."
    B. The right to adequate shelter is guaranteed by most states.
    C. Homeless people have the right to public assistance in the form of food stamps, disability benefits, and medical care.
    D. Some states have expanded how they define a "resident" of the state in order to ensure that the homeless can vote.

22. Which of the following would be classified by a social work practitioner, working in the dual perspective, as having a positive nurturing environment but a negative sustaining environment?

    A. A gay teenager who is rejected by his parents and by peers at school
    B. A minority child from a supportive home who feels marginalized in school
    C. A teenager from a supportive home who is sexually abused by an uncle
    D. A child who is abused by her parents but who has several close friends at school

23. A second-year social work student, an intern at a school, performs as a discussion-group leader for immigrant children. One of these children, a Filipino child, in response to a teacher's assignment to bring in a newspaper article, has brought in an article from a Tagalog newspaper. The teacher told the child mat he did not correctly complete his homework assignment The discussion leader's FIRST action should be to

    A. discuss the incident with a supervisor
    B. meet with the child and assure him that he did nothing wrong
    C. confront the teacher to discuss his or her cultural sensitivity
    D. plan a departmental seminar in cultural sensitivity

24. When an interviewer considers what type of nonverbal behavior will be appropriate given the interviewee's cultural background, the interviewer is making a decision about

    A. processing
    B. encoding
    C. decoding
    D. transmission

25. Which of the following is NOT a guideline to be followed in compiling a social history report?

    A. Avoid psychiatric labels and use behavioral examples instead.
    B. Numerous headings should be used to break information into topical categories.
    C. The report should be as comprehensive as possible.
    D. Label opinions and personal judgements as such.

26. In writing a social history report, the practitioner should focus as much as possible on

    A. resources and internal strengths that clients may use to address problems
    B. personal weaknesses and limitations that might impede progress
    C. environmental obstacles to change
    D. possible psychopathology

27. A client requests that a social worker help her figure out how to get money in order to purchase a car, because the client needs to get to and from a new job. The FIRST thing the worker should try to do is

    A. conduct a social history of the client
    B. help the client recognize the difference between means and ends
    C. challenge the client's motivation for buying a new car
    D. understand how expensive a car is to buy

28. During an interview, a general assistance client expresses frustration with the practitioner, and wonders aloud why he has to disclose so much information in order to get help. He makes the statement that social workers are all alike, and that all they know how to do is ask one question after another. In response to this, the MOST appropriate answer the practitioner can make is

    A. I don't like having to ask these questions any more than you like answering them.
    B. You think I ask too many questions?
    C. I'm sorry, but you'll have to provide this information if you expect any help.
    D. You're not making my job easy, either.

29. A social work supervisor sits down for an annual evaluation with a practitioner who is a counselor for sex-offenders. The greatest impediment to a fair evaluation of this person's demonstrated success is the

   A. tentative level of knowledge available to the practitioner in her work
   B. supervisor's lack of direct contacts with the counselor's clients
   C. extreme psychological strain involved in such work
   D. degree of specialization required by the field

30. The purpose of the _____ model of social work is to ensure that interventions give adequate and appropriate attention to the client's social environment, and to social change.

   A. task-centered
   B. interactional
   C. cognitive-behavioral
   D. structural

31. Which of the following is NOT an accurate description of a social worker/client relationship?

   A. Sympathetic
   B. Inherently unequal
   C. Purposeful
   D. Nonjudgemental

32. A social worker is fulfilling the role of a "broker" when he or she

   A. challenges an institution's decision not to provide services
   B. refers a physically abused wife to a shelter home
   C. helps a client to articulate his or her needs
   D. coordinates services from different agencies

33. First-order changes within a family typically affect

   A. communication patterns
   B. levels of pride or satisfaction
   C. role assignments
   D. shared worldview

34. Ethical difficulties with nonsexual dual relationships are most likely to occur in

   A. therapeutic settings
   B. community organizing
   C. mobilizing informal social support
   D. community development

35. Which of the following age groups leads the nation in percentage of suicides?

   A. 15- to 24-year-olds
   B. 25- to 40-year olds
   C. 40- to 64-year-olds
   D. 65 and older

36. In hiring preprofessional staff to work at a social services agency, administrators should consider their greatest benefit to be

A. greater flexibility in accepting difficult task assignments
B. substantial cost savings
C. improved understanding and relationships among clients
D. fresh insights and questioning mat may motivate change

37. Which of the following is NOT characteristic of a maladaptive defense to a set of stressors?

   A. reaction are generally passive
   B. patterns of behavior are stereotyped
   C. devised solutions are reality-oriented
   D. the reaction is unconscious

38. The "strength" of a particular behavior is commonly described in terms of each of the following, EXCEPT

   A. desirability
   B. intensity
   C. frequency
   D. duration

39. Which of the following is LEAST likely to be an indicator of child neglect?

   A. Poor school attendance
   B. Unsocialized eating habits
   C. Serious behavioral problems
   D. Voluntarily staying at school or in public places for extended periods

40. A social worker attempts to interview a young child who is believed to have suffered physical abuse. The worker notices that the child appears frightened, and says, "When I was your age, I was afraid to talk to people I didn't know that well." This is an example of the worker's attempt at

   A. parallelism
   B. encouragement
   C. normalization
   D. universalization

41. Which of the following is NOT a guideline to be used in writing intervention objectives?

   A. Compose two- or three-part objectives,
   B. Break down long-term objectives into ones with shorter time frames.
   C. Use positive ("will...") rather than negative ("will not...") language.
   D. Use behavioral language.

42. The NASW code states explicitly that a social worker has an ethical duty to
   I. take action against the incompetent practice of other social workers
   II. present materials at professional conferences and writing for professional journals
   III. protect the privacy of clients at all costs

   A. I and II
   B. I and III

C. II and III
D. I, II and III

43. In the helping continuum, which of the following types of support systems is most likely to occupy places on both the formal and informal ends of the spectrum?

    A. Professionals
    B. Mutual aid
    C. Self-help groups
    D. Assigned peer helpers

44. Which of the following is probably the BEST available method for a social worker to measure change's in a client's internal state?

    A. Time sampling
    B. Self-anchored rating scale
    C. Latency recording
    D. Frequency counting

45. Each of the following is a guideline for legislative advocacy at the state level of government, EXCEPT

    A. the advocate should press for open committee hearings on the bill
    B. support should be obtained from the governor and relevant state agencies, if possible
    C. the bill should be introduced toward the end of a legislative session
    D. the advocate should use the amendatory process as a strategy

46. In the ecological perspective of human behavior, the attributes of relatedness, competence, self-direction, and self-esteem can be described in each of the following ways, EXCEPT

    A. they appear to be interdependent
    B. they tend to develop at differential rates
    C. they appear to be relatively free of cultural bias
    D. they are outcomes of person/environment relationships

47. The "right to treatment" means that
    I. any person with mental illness may generally gain voluntary admission to an institution for treatment
    II. people with mental disabilities who do not live in an institution generally have rights to community-based services and treatment
    III. people who are involuntarily institutionalized for a mental illness generally have the right to a professionally acceptable treatment plan

    A. I and II
    B. II and III
    C. III only
    D. I, II and III

48. Which of the following ways of thinking about social work practice is most useful and most important during the beginning phases of the helping process?

    A. Feminist perspective
    B. Generalist perspective
    C. Task-centered model
    D. Behavioral theory

49. A worker believes that a client should change her approach toward her family, but does nothing to compel her to do so. Which of the following professional values or ethics is the worker implementing?

    A. Cultural sensitivity
    B. Self-determination
    C. Competence
    D. Dignity and respect

50. Male-dominated societies have been found by many researcher to have negative effects on men as well as women. These consequences include each of the following, EXCEPT

    A. homophobia
    B. restricted sexual behaviors
    C. restricted social mobility
    D. health care problems

KEY (CORRECT ANSWERS)

1. B	11. A	21. B	31. D	41. A
2. B	12. A	22. B	32. B	42. A
3. D	13. D	23. A	33. B	43. C
4. C	14. C	24. B	34. A	44. B
5. D	15. A	25. C	35. D	45. C
6. C	16. C	26. A	36. D	46. B
7. B	17. A	27. B	37. C	47. C
8. B	18. C	28. B	38. A	48. B
9. D	19. A	29. A	39. C	49. B
10. B	20. A	30. D	40. C	50. C

TEST 4

DIRECTIONS: Each question or incomplete statement is followed by several suggested answers or completions. Select the one the BEST answers the question or completes the statement. *PRINT THE LETTER OF THE CORRECT ANSWER IN THE SPACE AT THE RIGHT.*

Questions 51-54 refer to the genogram below.

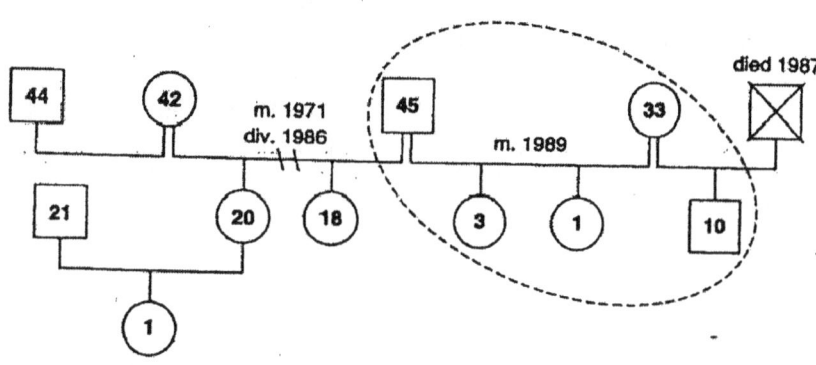

Based on the above genogram, classify each statement below as "True" or "False" in the blank next to each statement

1. The 10-year-old is from the mother's first marriage. 1.____

2. The 10-year-old lives with two stepsisters. 2.____

3. The 10-year-old's mother died in 1987. 3.____

4. The 10-year-old's stepfather is now a grandfather. 4.____

5. An aide assigned to a patient in a state mental hospital hears a complaint that the doctors and other staff have been treating him cruelly. The aide should FIRST 5.____

   A. try to persuade the doctors and staff to treat the patient better
   B. secure the patient's consent for filing a grievance
   C. find out what specific actions the patient felt were cruel
   D. determine the person to whom a grievance or complaint should be directed

6. Among the following ethnic minority groups in America, which is MOST likely to be open to help-seeking behaviors? 6.____

   A. Native Americans
   B. Latinos
   C. Jewish Americans
   D. African Americans

7. The major advantage associated with the use of commercially available data-gathering and assessment tools in social work is that they

   A. have already been field-tested
   B. are usually less costly than other measures
   C. are typically more focused and to-the-point in questioning
   D. involve broad applications

8. During an initial interview with a family of four, the social worker notices that the father and an adolescent son frequently interject with statements that are critical of the younger daughter's behavior. Each time one of them makes such a statement, the mother vigorously leaps to the daughter's defense. In her report, the social worker describes a pair of unhealthy alliances in the family system that have resulted in a split. In phrasing her assessment in this way, the worker is using the _____ approach.

   A. ecosystems
   B. functional
   C. structural
   D. psychodynamic

9. Indigenous nonprofessionals should be considered useful to a social services agency for each of the following reasons, EXCEPT

   A. willingness to undertake support functions at the agency
   B. serving as a communication channel between the organization and clients
   C. encouraging greater agency acceptance and credibility within the community
   D. helping the agency to accomplish meaningful change

10. Which of the following developmental tasks is most likely to be acquired by an individual between the ages of 13-17?

    A. Developing life-style apart from parents
    B. Abstract though processes
    C. Introspection
    D. Cooperation with others

11. According to Kadushin, the purpose of opening an initial client interview with general conversation or "small talk" is to

    A. construct an unobtrusive opportunity for making and recording initial observations
    B. ease the client's transition from a familiar mode of speaking into a new and unfamiliar role
    C. soften the client's defenses so that initial questioning will catch him/her off guard
    D. downplay the seriousness of the interview

12. The most significant difference between advocacy and other social service roles (brokerage, mediation, etc.) is that it

    A. is essentially a confrontation
    B. engages resources from different sectors of the community
    C. is directed outward
    D. cannot be accommodated by the ecosystems model

13. According to Warren, communities serve each of the following major functions, EXCEPT

    A. socialization
    B. mutual support
    C. protection from outsiders
    D. production/distribution/consumption

14. In the helping process, the social worker/client relationship may be appropriately used to
    I. convince the client of the importance of relying on others
    II. persuade a client to make necessary changes
    III. sustain clients as they work on the problem
    IV. serve as a model for other client interactions

    A. I, II and III
    B. II, III and IV
    C. III and IV
    D. I, II, III and IV

15. Which of the following stages of group development typically occurs FIRST?

    A. Power and control
    B. Differentiation
    C. Separation
    D. Intimacy

16. Each of the following is a general guideline that should be used for effective listening during the interview process, EXCEPT

    A. have a clear idea of the purpose of the interview before the session begins
    B. assume and accept a certain level of ignorance on the part of oneself
    C. develop a clear expectation about what the client will say during the interview
    D. listen for recurrent and dominant themes, rather than focus on detail

17. A child learns that her pet is called a "cat." Later, the child visits a friend's house and correctly identifies her friend's pet as a cat. According to Piaget, the child has achieved

    A. accommodation
    B. conservation
    C. assimilation
    D. object permanence

18. Which of the following statements about problem-solving planning for an agency is TRUE?

    A. Plans usually have a life span of 5 to 10 days.
    B. The need for it can be minimized with good operational or strategic planning.
    C. It is used primarily to address budget concerns.
    D. It is a proactive process.

19. A social worker wants to keep track of a client's eating behavior. Rather than have the client record the number of times he snacked between meals, the worker instructs the client to record the number of times he thought of snacking but didn't This strategy for measurement demonstrates the worker's sensitivity to _____ of a measurement.

A. reliability
B. sensitivity
C. reactivity
D. validity

20. When a family reports to a social work practitioner, each member of the family seems to focus his or her criticisms on the father, who is described in turn as uncooperative, unmotivated, and unyielding. Probably the best way for the practitioner to try to reframe this description is to say mat the father

    A. has a high regard for himself but a low regard for the opinions of others
    B. is a distraction to the others in their goal to achieve better communication
    C. has an unhealthy need to get his own way
    D. is assertive and logically resists doing things that don't make sense to him

21. The BEST description of the process involved in staff training in a social services agency is

    A. applying new knowledge to a problem situation
    B. instruction in and exposure to necessary knowledge
    C. providing knowledge that is generalizable
    D. provoking the exploration of different possible solutions

22. During an interview in which a social worker is attempting to assess a client's mental status, the worker focuses for a while on intellectual functioning-asking the client to read, write, follow simple instructions, and think abstractly. In assessing the client's intellectual functioning, it will be MOST important for the worker to consider the client's

    A. educational attainment
    B. affect
    C. cultural background
    D. recent medical history

23. Social learning theory proposes that some behaviors are learned by individuals through

    A. observation
    B. operant conditioning
    C. reinforcement
    D. classical conditioning

24. When confronted with a potential ethical conflict, a social worker following the ETHIC model of decision-making will FIRST consider

    A. how the standards of the NASW code, as well as relative laws and cases, apply to the situation
    B. the possible consequences of different decisions
    C. relevant personal, societal, agency, client and professional values
    D. who will benefit and who will be harmed by certain decisions

25. When interacting with a person who has a disability, general guidelines include 25.____
    I. Use a normal tone of voice when addressing visually impaired clients
    II. If the person is visually impaired or hard of hearing, avoid words such as "see" or "hear".
    III. If the person is deaf or hard of hearing, look directly at him or her when speaking, even if an interpreter is present.
    IV. In meeting or parting, shake whatever the person offers—hand, prosthesis, or elbow

   A. I and II
   B. I, III, and IV
   C. III and IV
   D. I, II, III and IV

KEY (CORRECT ANSWERS)

1.	True	11.	B
2.	True	12.	A
3.	False	13.	C
4.	True	14.	C
5.	C	15.	A
6.	C	16.	C
7.	A	17.	A
8.	C	18.	B
9.	A	19.	C
10.	B	20.	C

21. B
22. A
23. A
24. C
25. B

EXAMINATION SECTION
TEST 1

DIRECTIONS: Each question or incomplete statement is followed by several suggested answers or completions. Select the one the BEST answers the question or completes the statement. *PRINT THE LETTER OF THE CORRECT ANSWER IN THE SPACE AT THE RIGHT.*

1. The primary sources of data in most assessments are

    A. completed assessment forms
    B. the client's verbal statements
    C. psychological test results
    D. collateral sources

2. A social worker is fulfilling the role of a "mediator" when he or she

    A. calls attention to the probable social consequences to a new housing development
    B. refers a jobless person to an unemployment agency
    C. evaluates the outcome of a colleague's practice
    D. helps a frustrated wife to clarify her position to a husband

3. In the systems model of human behavior, "division of labor" is an example of

    A. autopoiesis
    B. social control
    C. differentiation
    D. hierarchy

4. After several weeks of behavioral intervention, a child is consistently performing the desired behavior targeted by his parents and a social worker: that is, he is going to bed at the correct time without argument or delaying tactics. Now that he's reached this stage, the social worker recommends that the parents gradually withdraw the prompts and reinforcements that induced the behavior to begin with. This is an example of

    A. extinction
    B. shaping
    C. fading
    D. modeling

5. When working with a group, a social worker encourages decision-making by consensus. Drawbacks to the use of consensus include

    A. involvement of few available group resources
    B. alienation of the minority
    C. time- and energy-intensiveness
    D. decreased likelihood of handling future controversies

6. The primary rationale for the use of a social history for client assessment is that

    A. past behavior is the best predictor of future behavior
    B. the best source of information about a client's situation is the client her/himself
    C. the best protection against legal liability is an exhaustive data set

D. problems exist because of an unbalanced reaction between a client system and the environment

7. Most professional codes of ethics provide that a social worker's primary ethical duty is to

   A. respect client privacy and confidentiality
   B. challenge social injustice
   C. work in the best interest of clients
   D. avoid situations that involve ethical conflicts

8. In agency planning, which of the following visual aids will be MOST useful in helping to examine the benefits and drawbacks of different alternative choices

   A. Task planning sheet
   B. Gantt chart
   C. Decision tree
   D. PERT chart

9. Which of the following questions or statements is MOST appropriate for a practitioner in initiating an interview?

   A. "I understand you have a problem."
   B. "You came in here to see me about _____."
   C. "How can I help you today?"
   D. "I'm glad you came in to see me

10. What is the term commonly used to describe children who suffer physical, mental, or emotional injuries inflicted by caretaking adults?

    A. Developmentally disabled
    B. Victims
    C. At risk
    D. Abused or neglected

11. Typically, the questioning process in a social work interview should progress

    A. chronologically
    B. from general to specific
    C. from specific to general
    D. in a series of grouped topical units

12. Assessment is a process that is considered to be the task of the

    A. agency psychiatrist or clinician
    B. social worker
    C. client
    D. social worker and client together

13. A social worker who wants to use a small group as a resource for clients should remember the general rule that the addition of new members, especially resistant ones, should be avoided during the _____ stage of group development.

    A. differentiation
    B. intimacy

C. preaffiliation
D. power and control

14. During an assessment interview with a male high school student, it becomes clear to the practitioner that the boy's behavior problems are related in some way to his frustration at the different expectations of his teachers and his peers concerning the role of a student. The boy is experiencing

    A. inter-role conflict
    B. role ambiguity
    C. intra-role conflict
    D. role incapacity

15. When considering the use of informal resources for an intervention, the social worker should

    A. view informal resources as an inexpensive alternative to formal services
    B. whenever possible, try to "professionalize" or train informal resources to lend them authority
    C. already have some knowledge of available self-help groups in the community
    D. whenever informal resources are identified, try to steer clients toward the ones that are probably most useful

16. Probably the biggest difference between the supervisory role in social work and that of other professions is the

    A. amount of psychological support that must be provided to supervisees
    B. degree of direct involvement in the work of supervisees
    C. predominant use of "soft" criteria in performance evaluations
    D. greater difficulty in matching workers to tasks

17. A social worker is interviewing a woman in a mental hospital who appears lucid but is suspected of having some mental illness. When gathering information, the worker should

    A. explain fully the reason for the interview and ask the client to give her opinion of her mental status
    B. ask short, closed-ended assessment questions up front
    C. administer a standardized assessment that may be evaluated by a psychologist
    D. work assessment questions into the ordinary flow of the conversation

18. A social worker becomes aware of a colleague's incompetent or unethical practice. According to the NASW code, the worker's FIRST obligation is to

    A. inform all of the colleague's relevant clients of the situation
    B. approach the colleague to discuss his/her incapacitation, incompetence, etc.
    C. file a complaint with the NASW
    D. file a complaint with the appropriate licensing board

19. A "communication loop" is completed when

    A. the person to whom the message is addressed begins to respond
    B. the person who initiates the message has completed the transmission
    C. the person to whom the message is addressed receives the message
    D. the person to whom the message is addressed decodes the message

20. Because many parents believe in and utilize corporal punishment as discipline, a social worker must be able to differentiate physical abuse from ordinary spanking or corporal punishment. Which of the following is NOT a useful means of making this distinction?

    A. Parent striking the child in places that are easily injured
    B. Repeated episodes of corporal punishment
    C. Child's report that punishments are severe and painful
    D. Injury to child's body tissue

21. A social worker makes an initial in-home visit to a married couple who have willingly submitted to an intervention regarding their marital problems. During the interview the couple points out that they will be leaving the area in a few weeks, because the wife has been transferred by her employer to a new location. Probably the MOST appropriate plan for dealing with this couple would involve the _____ model of social work.

    A. person-centered
    B. cognitive-behavioral
    C. solution-focused
    D. task-centered

22. The primary purpose of evaluative research in social work is to

    A. measure a client's self-satisfaction
    B. determine whether outcomes can be attributed to an intervention
    C. express the effectiveness of interventions in material terms
    D. determine whether an outcome was achieved

23. Each of the following should be used as a guideline in child placement decisions, EXCEPT

    A. efforts to protect the child should involve as little disruption as possible
    B. use of placement to compel a parent to take some action
    C. involvement of parents and child in the placement decision
    D. maintenance of child's cultural beliefs in placement

24. Which of the following is NOT a factor involved in the decoding of a message?

    A. Relationship with interviewer
    B. Social, emotional, and cognitive barriers
    C. Ethics
    D. Context of interview

25. A practitioner wants to make the parents of an adolescent aware of the behavioral manifestations of depression. Which of the following is LEAST likely to be an indicator?

    A. Sudden tearful reactions
    B. Excessive pleasure-seeking
    C. Decline in school achievement
    D. Jokes about death or dying

26. Which of the following is LEAST likely to be an area of conflict between social workers and attorneys

A. Confidentiality
B. Recording information
C. The best interests of a client
D. The definition of "client"

27. Which of the following typically occurs in the first stage of group therapy?

    A. The members are hostile toward the leader.
    B. Cliques form within the group.
    C. The members talk through the leader and seem to ignore one another.
    D. The members interact with each other tend to ignore the leader.

28. In conducting employee evaluations, a social work supervisor should use _____ as available criteria.
    I. pre-established objective measures such as timeliness
    II. "soft" criteria such as attitude
    III. the supervisor's own work experience
    IV. the performance of others in similar assignments

    A. I only
    B. I and II
    C. I and III
    D. I, II, III and IV

29. Which of the following is NOT a term that is interchangeable with "stepfamily"?

    A. Remarried family
    B. Blended family
    C. Reconstituted family
    D. Renested family

30. A worker refers a client to a colleague who specializes and is trained in law, even though the client requested the service from the worker. Which of the following professional values or ethics is the worker implementing?

    A. Self-determination
    B. Privacy
    C. Competence
    D. Confidentiality

31. Social work practice that is based on behavioral theory assumes that behaviors are determined by

    A. emotions
    B. consequences
    C. values
    D. internal thought processes

32. Which of the following is NOT a symptom associated with bipolar disorder?

    A. Increase in goal-oriented activity
    B. Distractibility
    C. Significant weight loss
    D. Decreased need for sleep

33. A 'helping relationship" between the social worker and client is BEST described as

   A. the goal of any initial contact between worker and client
   B. the medium offered to people in trouble through which they are presented with opportunities
   C. the means by which a worker gains the client's trust to solve problems
   D. a lifeline that is thrown to people in trouble in order to help them out of current problems

34. Communities often contain individuals who are categorized as "AFDC mothers" or "hardcore unemployed" or "AIDS patients," among others. This is a destructive application of the concept of

   A. service delivery
   B. niche
   C. differentiation
   D. diversity

35. The first step in any single-system practice evaluation is to

   A. record baseline data
   B. select suitable measures
   C. implement the intervention
   D. specify the goal

36. A social worker plans a behavioral intervention for a developmentally disabled adult who does not look people in the eye when speaking with them.
   Each of the following behavioral strategies may be useful to the intervention, EXCEPT

   A. overcorrection
   B. instruction
   C. prompting
   D. shaping

37. During several in-home visits with a family, the mother repeatedly refuses to acknowledge that her alcoholism is having an adverse effect on others in the household. The MOST appropriate next step for the social worker would be to initiate

   A. a challenge
   B. behavioral rehearsal
   C. self-talk management
   D. a behavioral contract

38. Working-class or low-income marriages are typically characterized by

   A. marriage late in life
   B. flexible divisions of labor
   C. troubled mother-child relationships
   D. emotional distance between partners

39. A researcher repeatedly measures the dependent variable throughout two baseline and two treatment phases of a study to assess whether variability in the dependent variable is due to the influence of the independent variable. She is using a(n) _____ design of measurement.

A. AB
B. ABAB
C. multiple baseline
D. Solomon four-group

40. What is the typical time-frame for crisis intervention?

    A. One to two weeks
    B. Six to eight weeks
    C. At least eight weeks
    D. Six months or more, depending on the nature of the crisis

41. Stigma, once it has become part of a culture, has certain predictable consequences. Which of the following is NOT one of these consequences?

    A. Discrimination
    B. Absorption
    C. Altered self-concept
    D. Development of subculture

42. A social worker is engaged in a one-on-one interview with a 10-year-old boy, in order to investigate allegations of a father's sexual abuse. The allegations were initially brought by the mother, now divorced from the father, and were later corroborated by the boy. The mother and father are engaged in a custody battle for the boy. The boy's account of events is extremely consistent over time, listing the same major events in sequence, but his affect is flat—he relates his accounts of abuse in an oddly detached manner. The BEST action for the social worker at this point would be to

    A. terminate the interview and begin criminal proceedings against the father
    B. terminate the interview and refer the child for an immediate psychiatric consultation
    C. ask the mother to join in the interview and see if her account matches the boy's
    D. ask the boy to go into greater detail about the related events, out of sequence, and then repeat the request at a later time

43. When working with individuals or families of native American cultures, it is best to begin by

    A. gathering a social history
    B. using indirect approaches such as analogy or metaphor
    C. asking for open-ended descriptions of family roles
    D. direct questioning

44. In cases of elder abuse, the government may intervene if
    I. the older person requests it
    II. the older person is found at a hearing to be incompetent
    III. the abuse or neglect presents an unacceptable level of danger to the older person
    IV. the abuse is properly reported and recorded by a visiting social services worker

    A. I only
    B. I and II

C. I, II and III
D. I, II, III and IV

45. Which of the following is a guideline that should be observed in developing an assessment questionnaire for clients?

    A. Develop several focused questionnaires rather than a single all-purpose one.
    B. The most sensitive or probing questions should appear near the middle of the questionnaire.
    C. For complex ideas, form two-part questions.
    D. Include only open-ended questions.

46. During the assessment phase of an interview, checklists are most useful for identifying and selecting

    A. problems for intervention
    B. specific objectives
    C. available resources
    D. general goals

47. Which of the following is an advantage associated with the family life-cycle model?

    A. It highlights the special challenges of blended families.
    B. It identifies developmental tasks for families at specific stages.
    C. It is especially applicable to families in minority groups.
    D. It applies to those who do not have children.

48. Before making the decision to advocate on behalf of a client, it is important to consider several factors. Which of the following is NOT one of these?

    A. Client's consent for advocacy.
    B. Whether advocating is the most useful process that can be applied to the situation.
    C. Whether the complaint or decision involves a legitimate grievance
    D. Client's knowledge and feeling about human services.

49. Which of the following is an advantage associated with the use of genograms in client assessment?

    A. Targeting and identification of relevant social supports.
    B. Execution and interpretation require no instruction.
    C. Placement of an individual or family within a social context.
    D. A considerable shortening of the case record.

50. Activities involved in social casework typically include

    A. counseling those with a terminal illness
    B. supervising juvenile probation clients
    C. providing job training
    D. preparing court reports

51. In middle childhood, school-age children are generally concerned with

    A. "good" behavior in order to receive approval from others
    B. behaving appropriately because they fear punishment

C. the concordance of behaviors with an adopted moral code
D. conforming with group standards in order to be rewarded

52. When a social worker/client relationship is characterized by ineffectiveness, the most common reason is that

A. resources are not available to meet the client's needs
B. the client has not sufficiently specified his or her needs
C. an incorrect solution has been identified by the worker
D. the worker is attempting to keep the relationship on a pleasant level

53. A social history report includes the statement: "The subject claims to have completed high school." This should be included under the heading:

A. Family Background and Situation
B. Intellectual functioning
C. Impressions and Assessment
D. Such a statement shouldn't appear at all in a social history report.

54. According to Erickson, which of the following stages of psychosocial development occurs FIRST in the human life span?

A. Initiative vs. guilt
B. Trust vs. mistrust
C. Identity vs. role confusion
D. Autonomy vs. shame and doubt

55. The strategy of "reframing" is most useful for

A. desensitizing clients to past trauma
B. classifying client/family problems according to standard diagnostic categories
C. helping clients to model their own behavior after others'
D. revealing a client's strengths and opportunities for helping

56. In general, it is believed that interviewers who spend less than a minimum of _____ of an interview listening to the client are more active than they should be.

A. one-fourth
B. one-third
C. one-half
D. two thirds

57. In the _____ model of social work, the goal of the social worker is to enhance and restore the psychosocial functioning of persons, or to change noxious social conditions that impede the mutually beneficial interaction between person and their environment.

A. structural-functional
B. ecological
C. medical
D. strategic

58. In social work, "micro" practice usually focuses on

   A. resolving the problems of individuals, families, or small groups
   B. planning, administration, evaluation, and community organizing
   C. developmental activities in the social environment
   D. facilitating communication, mediation, and negotiation

59. _____ theory may prove most productive for the social work practitioner in understanding families of homosexuals, because it introduces unambiguous distinctions between stigma and homosexual behaviors and feelings.

   A. Structural
   B. Object relations
   C. Strategic
   D. Labeling

60. A client tells a practitioner that his main goal for intervention is to decide on a college major. To BEST help this client, the practitioner will assume the role of

   A. enabler
   B. mediator
   C. initiator
   D. educator

61. Which of the following is NOT a guideline for interacting with clients from a Latino culture?

   A. Efforts to foster independence and self-reliance may be interpreted by many Latinos as a lack of concern for others.
   B. Efforts to deal one-on-one with an adolescent client may serve to alienate the parents, especially the mother.
   C. A nonverbal gesture such as lowering the eyes is interpreted by many Latinos as a sign of respect and deference to authority.
   D. In much of Latino culture, the locus of control for problems tends to be much more external than internal.

62. The broadest, most general type of plan used in social work administration is the

   A. plan for meeting objectives
   B. statement of goals
   C. statement of mission
   D. guiding policies

63. In composing a social network grid with a client, which of the following steps is typically performed FIRST?

   A. Dividing acquaintances according to direction of help
   B. Dividing acquaintances according to duration of acquaintance
   C. Identifying people who can help the client in concrete ways
   D. Identifying areas of life in which people impact the client

64. An administrator notices, in several trips through the agency grounds, that a handful of the organization's support staff are often engaged in socializing or other nonproductive activities. The groups are always small and never made up of the same people, and nearly all members of the support staff have received satisfactory evaluations from their supervisor. The socializing does not occur around clients or visiting professionals. Over the past several years, the agency's efficiency record has remained about the same. The agency would probably be BEST served by the view that

   A. rigid controls should be implemented to reduce this behavior
   B. a memorandum should be circulated citing this behavior as a poor example
   C. the behavior may help to relieve boredom and should be ignored
   D. the supervisor should add an item or two to the evaluation that will address this behavior

65. Each of the following is a stage of the dying process described by Kübler-Ross, EXCEPT

   A. acknowledgement
   B. depression
   C. anger
   D. acceptance

66. For a prison inmate, "notice of rights" means the inmate
   I. receives advance notice of what conduct will result in discipline or punishment
   II. receives written notice of any charges against him
   III. is entitled to organize a group meeting for political purposes

   A. I and II
   B. I and III
   C. II and III
   D. I, II and III

67. Which of the following values is NOT generally indigenous to families of Asian heritage?

   A. Inconspicuousness
   B. Perfectionism
   C. Fatalism
   D. Shame as a behavioral influence

68. Most professionals recommend that in order to accurately evaluate the effect of an intervention, baseline data should be collected for no fewer than _____ data points.

   A. 2
   B. 3
   C. 4
   D. 5

69. During an assessment interview, a social worker and a client try to clarify and analyze the client's sense of self. If the worker wants to discover something about the client's self-acceptance, which of the following questions is MOST appropriate?

   A. To what extent do you worry about illness and physical incapacity?
   B. Is what you expect to happen mostly good or mostly bad?

C. Do you enjoy the times when you are alone?
D. Where do your other family members live?

70. Which of the following cognitive traits explains the mistaken belief held by many adolescents that they are invincible or protected from harmful consequences of their behavior?

    A. The personal fable
    B. Object delusion
    C. Egocentrism
    D. Pseudohypocrisy

71. An 18-year-old woman comes to see a social worker at a crisis center one day after being raped on a date. In the interview with this client, the social worker should FIRST:

    A. emphasize medical and legal procedures
    B. obtain factual information about the rape
    C. listen to the client and support her emotionally
    D. help the client establish contact with significant others

72. During a client assessment, each of the following should be considered a useful question, EXCEPT

    A. Can you tell me about times when you've successfully handled a problem like this in the past?
    B. When family members complain about your behavior, what to they say?
    C. How have you managed to cope up to this point?
    D. What do your friends and family seem to like most about you?

73. Norms are MOST accurately described as

    A. attitudes toward life events and processes
    B. assumptions about the world
    C. expectations of the self and others
    D. ideas about what is proper and desirable behavior

74. Generally, when a homeless person or group is removed from a condemned or abandoned property under the law, the most significant legal question to arise is whether

    A. the last owner of the property can be located for consent
    B. the property is being "rehabilitated" by the occupants
    C. the state recognizes a "right to shelter"
    D. the property has really been abandoned

75. A social worker introduces herself to a family household in which an elderly man lives. The man has been reported by neighbors on several occasions for making threats of violence to a number of adolescents in the neighborhood. The worker recognizes that she is uninvited, and the BEST way for her to describe the purpose of her relationship to the family would be as

A. helping the man to modify his behavior so that no further institutional involvement will be necessary
B. helping the man to avoid the aggravating stimulus of contact with neighborhood teens
C. protecting the neighborhood from the elderly man's threats
D. arranging for the man to get counseling in order to understand and change his behavior

---

KEY (CORRECT ANSWERS)

1. B	16. A	31. B	46. D	61. D
2. D	17. D	32. C	47. B	62. C
3. C	18. B	33. B	48. D	63. D
4. C	19. A	34. B	49. D	64. C
5. C	20. C	35. D	50. A	65. A
6. A	21. C	36. A	51. A	66. A
7. C	22. B	37. A	52. D	67. B
8. C	23. B	38. D	53. D	68. B
9. B	24. C	39. B	54. B	69. C
10. B	25. B	40. B	55. D	70. A
11. B	26. C	41. B	56. D	71. C
12. D	27. C	42. D	57. B	72. B
13. D	28. B	43. B	58. A	73. D
14. C	29. D	44. B	59. D	74. B
15. C	30. C	45. A	60. A	75. A

TEST 2

DIRECTIONS: Each question or incomplete statement is followed by several suggested answers or completions. Select the one that BEST answers the question or completes the statement. *PRINT THE LETTER OF THE CORRECT ANSWER IN THE SPACE AT THE RIGHT.*

1. A 24-year-old mother of four, recently widowed, tells a practitioner: "I feel like my whole life has just fallen apart. I don't think I can take care of my family on my own. My husband always made all the decisions and earned the money to support us. I haven't slept well since he died and I've started drinking more often. My parents try to help me but it's not enough."
   The practitioner responds by saying: "So you're afraid about your ability to shoulder all the family responsibilities now." This response is an example of a(n)

   A. reflection
   B. clarification
   C. paraphrase
   D. summarization

2. At the beginning of an intake interview, a social worker's tasks are to
   I. gather data and conduct an assessment
   II. establish a positive relationship with the interviewee
   III. obtain brief details that will indicate whether the situation for which the client wants help is among the problems for which the worker offers help
   IV. offer help

   A. I only
   B. I and II
   C. II and III
   D. I, II, III and IV

3. Which of the following is NOT a basic purpose of a professional code of ethics?

   A. To provide a mechanism for professional accountability
   B. To educate professionals about sound conduct
   C. To set standards that will be understood and enforced across all cultures
   D. To serve as a tool for improving practice

4. According to cognitive-behavioral theory, schemas represent a client's

   A. subversive attempts to persist in faulty cognitions
   B. automatic responses
   C. different response patterns
   D. core beliefs and assumptions

5. Objective data found in a client's folder might include

   A. A neighbor's recorded statement about a previous incident
   B. Notes on an interview with his psychotherapist
   C. A work evaluation performed by a supervisor
   D. A summary of previous criminal convictions

6. In the middle phase of a client interview, as a problem is being further explored, the practitioner should spend a considerable amount of time

   A. interpreting behavior
   B. confronting discrepancies
   C. restating or paraphrasing
   D. negotiating a service contract

7. Which of the following statements is TRUE about social work assessment?

   A. It is another term for "goal setting."
   B. It identifies a problem and its potential impact.
   C. It refers to the search for alternative solutions.
   D. It relates to the evaluation of program effectiveness.

8. An agency needs to write a proposal to a private foundation in order to request funding for renovations. It will be necessary for the agency to organize a _____ group.

   A. training
   B. task-focused
   C. recreation
   D. self-help

9. Social exchange theory is based on the idea that people

   A. often attempt to superimpose their own needs onto the desires of others
   B. aim to protect themselves from punishment in relationships
   C. aim to maximize rewards and minimize costs in relationships
   D. exchange rewards with those who are most like themselves

10. Privileged communication typically applies in cases of
    I. marital infidelity, if both spouses are participating in treatment
    II. legal proceedings in which a practitioner is asked to produce client records in court
    III. child abuse or neglect
    IV. client disclosures of personal and sensitive information

    A. I and III
    B. I, II and IV
    C. III and IV
    D. I, II, III and IV

11. During an assessment interview, a practitioner asks questions about the client's customs and traditions. The practitioner is most likely seeking information about the impact of _____ on the client's functioning.

    A. unhealthy patterns
    B. self-talk
    C. interpersonal relationships
    D. cultural diversity

12. Each of the following is true of the intervention phase of social work, EXCEPT that it

    A. is focused on problems
    B. requires interviewing, recording, letter writing, and referral skills
    C. is guided by the principles of self-determination and acceptance
    D. results naturally from a thorough assessment

13. During a client interview, a practitioner is attempting to summarize what the client has just said, but the client gives signs that he does not agree with the summary and intends to interrupt. The practitioner believes it is important for the client to hear how the summary sounds in someone else's words. In order to maintain his turn at speaking, the practitioner may want to

    A. raise an index finger
    B. raise his eyebrows
    C. speak more loudly
    D. stop all accompanying gestures and body movements

14. In Erikson's model of human development, the stage at which a child learns to meet the demands of society is

    A. identity vs. role confusion
    B. industry vs. inferiority
    C. basic trust vs. mistrust
    D. autonomy vs. shame and doubt

15. Generally, controlled experimental designs account for about_____ percent of all social work research.

    A. 5
    B. 20
    C. 35
    D. 55

16. What is the term for a social work process that brings an intervention to a close?

    A. Recognizing success
    B. Integrating gains
    C. Terminating the relationship
    D. Expanding opportunities

17. Which of the following is an example of primary prevention for mental illness?

    A. Crisis intervention
    B. Parent-child communication training
    C. Psychotherapy
    D. Teacher referrals to social workers of children targeted by bullies

18. Which of the following is an example of a closed question?

    A. How do you think you can, as you've said, 'Come more alive?'
    B. Of all the problems we've discussed, which bothers you the most?
    C. What is your relationship with your family?
    D. What kinds of things do you find yourself longing for?

19. Over time, adult personalities are likely to change in each of the following ways, EXCEPT becoming more

    A. candid
    B. dependable
    C. receptive to the company of others
    D. accepting of hardship

19.____

20. Which of the following BEST describes the mission of social work?

    A. Meeting client needs while influencing social institutions to become more responsive to people
    B. Helping clients negotiate an often complex and difficult network of services
    C. Constantly responding and adapting to social changes in micro and macro environments
    D. Identifying programs and connecting clients to needed services

20.____

21. Numerous studies have been conducted to determine which factors in a client/helping professional relationship are consistently related to positive outcomes. Which of the following is/are NOT one of these conditions?

    A. A relationship analogous to doctor/patient
    B. Empathy and positive regard
    C. A working alliance
    D. Transference and countertransference

21.____

22. A person who donates anonymously to a favorite charity is most likely driven by what Maslow called

    A. intrinsic motivation
    B. extrinsic motivation
    C. affective habituation
    D. self-actualization

22.____

23. According to the NASW code of ethics, sexual contact between practitioners and former clients is

    A. strongly discouraged under any circumstances
    B. discouraged, but considered acceptable if it occurs two years or more after the professional relationship has been terminated
    C. grounds for expulsion from the social work profession
    D. a private matter whose nature is left entirely up to the practitioner and the client

23.____

24. During an unstructured interview with a client, a practitioner generally focuses on

    A. discovering the presenting problem
    B. confronting erroneous self-talk
    C. giving reflective responses that elicit more information
    D. a prescribed list of screening questions

24.____

25. Process recording is an assessment technique that is most often used in

    A. clinical settings
    B. family sculpting

25.____

C. one-on-one interviews
D. group sessions

26. The NASW's stance on bartering with clients, rather than simply charging fees for service, includes the opinion that social workers should
    I. participate in barter in only in very limited circumstances
    II. ensure that such arrangements are an accepted practice among professionals in the local community
    III. propose bartering if it is clear the client will be unable to pay for services
    IV. never barter with clients under any circumstances

    A. I only
    B. I and II
    C. I, II and III
    D. IV only

27. Etiquette, customs, and minor regulations are examples of

    A. mores
    B. norms
    C. ethics
    D. folkways

28. A practitioner working in the Adlerian model is likely to use each of the following as an assessment instrument, EXCEPT

    A. personality inventories
    B. ecomaps
    C. lifestyle inventories
    D. early childhood recollections

29. Which of the following information would typically be solicited at the LATEST point in an intake interview?

    A. educational history
    B. family/marital/sexual history
    C. vocational history
    D. past interventions or service requests

30. According to conflict theorists, the "hidden curriculum" of schools

    A. serves to transmit different cultural values
    B. encourages social integration
    C. often results in self-fulfilling prophecy
    D. perpetuates existing social inequalities

31. The high value placed on individual freedom in American society has arguably produced each of the following, EXCEPT

    A. a cultural paradox
    B. an environmental dilemma
    C. unfair economic competition
    D. a *caveat emptor* ("let the buyer beware") approach to the market economy

32. One model of the relationship between helping professionals and clients emphasizes the social influence of professionals in counseling roles. To be effective, practitioners in the counseling role can draw on a power base that arises out of the relationship with the client. In client relationships, the power base that is typically LEAST helpful for the practitioner is known as _____ power.

    A. referent
    B. expert
    C. legitimate
    D. reward

33. In social work, experimental research designs

    A. are the most commonly conducted form of social work research
    B. obligate the researcher to offer a treatment to a control group as soon as possible after the study is terminated
    C. are usually single-system designs
    D. are generally free of ethical concerns if the research is conducted well

34. The term "social stratification" refers to social inequality that is

    A. differential
    B. structured
    C. institutionally sanctioned
    D. imperceptible

35. To a practitioner working from the behavioral perspective, the most important feature of good relationships is

    A. effective coping behaviors
    B. freedom from conflict
    C. complementary needs
    D. well-established boundaries

36. In an initial interview, it is common for clients to

    A. break down emotionally
    B. describe problems in a way that minimizes their own contributions to them
    C. disclose very personal information and emotions
    D. be someone other than the person who has arranged the interview

37. Which of the following is NOT a trend in the use of family approaches in direct social work practice?

    A. Increased attention on the family as an isolated system
    B. Increased attention to family diversity
    C. The use of a variety of social science theoretical approaches
    D. The use of multiple intervention models

38. The process whereby a client's place past feelings or attitudes toward significant people in their lives onto their social work practitioner is known as

    A. transference
    B. denial

C. countertransference
D. projection

39. Social desirability bias often causes people to

    A. make appraisals of others that are based on their social functioning rather than their effectiveness in other roles
    B. attribute their successes to skill, while blaming external factors for failures
    C. modify their responses to surveys or interviews based on what they think are desirable responses
    D. focus on the style of their interactions with others, rather than the substance

40. A social worker attends an evening anniversary party at which she has consumed some alcohol, which she rarely drinks. She doesn't think she is literally drunk, but would acknowledge feeling slightly tipsy and perhaps not in full command of herself. When she arrives at home later, she listens to a message from a client that was left on her answering machine while she was out. The client, with whom she has met several times, is feeling lonely and desperate because of the recent loss of his wife to cancer. The social worker wants to help. She should

    A. return the call immediately and try to counsel the client
    B. return the call immediately and explain that she is unable to help right now, but will call first thing tomorrow
    C. avoid contacting the client until she has recovered her ability to perform up to her usual professional standards and judgement
    D. contact a trusted colleague, give him or her the relevant information, and ask that he or she try to counsel the client over the phone

41. During an assessment interview, a practitioner asks a client: "What kinds of feelings do you have when this happens to you?" The practitioner is trying to identify the _____ associated with the problem.

    A. affect and mood states
    B. secondary gains
    C. overt behaviors or motoric responses
    D. internal dialogue

42. Hospital social workers typically engage in each of the following types of interventions or practice, EXCEPT

    A. crisis intervention
    B. discharge planning
    C. long-term counseling
    D. group work

43. For social work practitioners, symptoms of "burnout" on the job typically include each of the following, EXCEPT

    A. feeling unable to accomplish goals
    B. emotional exhaustion
    C. chronic worry
    D. a feeling of detachment from clients and work

44. When a case manager reaches the point in service coordination during which he makes a referral, he has assumed the role of

    A. evaluator
    B. broker
    C. advocate
    D. planner

45. A practitioner encounters a situation in which his own personal values conflict with a client's. In this instance, the practitioner is expected to engage in

    A. peer review
    B. value suspension
    C. legal consultation
    D. value clarification

46. Among the following American groups, the women who have the greatest risk of HIV infection are

    A. white
    B. African American
    C. Native American
    D. Hispanic

47. The trend in school social work has been a gradual shift toward an emphasis on the _____ perspective.

    A. behavioral
    B. input-based
    C. ecological
    D. psychiatric

48. The success of client-written logs as an assessment tool may depend on the client's motivation to keep a log. Which of the following is LEAST likely to help motivate a client to keep a log?

    A. Establishing a clear rationale or purpose for keeping the log
    B. Establishing negative consequences if the client fails to make log entries
    C. Adapting the log type to the client's abilities to self-monitor
    D. Involving the client in discussing and analyzing the log

49. The social work value of *empathy* is defined as a practitioner's capacity to

    A. imagine oneself in another's situation
    B. feel compassion for a person who is in distress
    C. convince a person that things will get better
    D. make a person recognize his/her own inner strength

50. Focusing on a client's positive assets and strengths during an assessment interview
    I. emphasizes the wholeness of the client system, rather than simply the problematic aspects
    II. gives a practitioner information about potential problems that might arise during an intervention
    III. helps convey to the client that they have internal resources that may prove useful
    IV. risks skewing the effectiveness of an intervention by taking the focus off the presenting problem

    A. I and III
    B. I, II and III
    C. III only
    D. I, II, III and IV

51. A hospital social worker is meeting with an 86-year-old man who suffers from Alzheimer's disease. His symptoms thus far have consisted largely of incidents of forgetfulness, and he has shown no signs of dementia or violence. The client's daughter, who has recently succeeded in having her father grant her a power of attorney over his affairs. When the social worker asks questions of the client, the daughter repeated breaks in and attempts to answer for him, though he appears to be lucid. When the social worker asks to speak to the client alone, the daughter refuses. The social worker should

    A. suspect a case of elder abuse and contact the adult protective services agency to look into it
    B. pretend to leave, and then attempt to interview the man when the daughter leaves the room
    C. suspect that the daughter may have suffered abuse at the hands of her father and adult protective services to look into it
    D. suspect a case of elder abuse and contact local law enforcement authorities

52. Which of the following is a key element of the case management paradigm?

    A. A focus on improving the quality and accessibility of resources
    B. A focus on developing vocational adjustment
    C. The selection of interventions based on empirical research
    D. Rational-emotive therapy

53. Of the following health problems, each affects the elderly to a greater extent than other age groups. The one that leads by the greatest percentage is

    A. cancer
    B. stroke
    C. heart disease
    D. Alzheimer's disease

54. Approximately _____ of all direct practice interventions are terminated because of unanticipated situational factors.

    A. an eighth
    B. a quarter
    C. half
    D. three-quarters

55. Social factors that increase the risk for suicide include each of the following, EXCEPT that the person

    A. lives alone
    B. has repeatedly rejected support
    C. has no ongoing therapeutic relationship
    D. is married

55.____

56. Practitioners are generally considered to have an ethical obligation to do each of the following, EXCEPT

    A. remain aware of their own values
    B. seek to learn about the diverse cultural backgrounds of their clients
    C. avoid imposing their values on clients
    D. refer clients whose values strongly differ from their own

56.____

57. Studies of young people who join urban gangs suggests that most often, people join gangs because of a need for a(n)

    A. peer group
    B. outlet for pent-up aggression and frustration
    C. surrogate family
    D. vehicle for criminal activity

57.____

58. After terminating a working relationship with a social worker, a client joins the local chapter of Alcoholics Anonymous. In doing so, she is attempting to

    A. form new therapeutic relationships
    B. prolong treatment
    C. maintain gains
    D. generalize gains

58.____

59. A key concept of narrative therapy is the idea tha

    A. clients often construct one-dimensional stories that don't tell the whole truth
    B. clearly naming a problem or disorder is the first step in solving it
    C. problems are inseparable from the person
    D. interventions are narrowly targeted to "revisions" of specific passages within the story

59.____

60. The creation of social service programs typically accomplishes each of the following, EXCEPT

    A. prevention
    B. enhancement
    C. retrenchment
    D. remediation

60.____

61. The most significant health problem facing Native Americans today is

    A. tuberculosis
    B. alcoholism
    C. heart disease
    D. diabetes

61.____

62. Which of the following is NOT one of the six "core values" that is cited in the preamble to the NASW's code of ethics?

   A. Service
   B. Confidentiality
   C. Integrity
   D. Importance of human relationships

63. Each of the following is a guideline for a practitioner's participation in crisis intervention procedures, EXCEPT

   A. expressing empathy by saying things such as "I understand"
   B. asking the client to describe the event
   C. letting the client talk for as long as he or she likes without interruption
   D. asking the client to describe his or her reactions and responses

64. A practitioner has begun to work with clients in one-on-one settings. He thinks perhaps self-disclosure would be a good way to establish a solid, caring relationship with his clients. He should remember that in working with clients professionally, there will always be a tension between the competing forces of self-disclosure and

   A. candor
   B. liability
   C. reciprocity
   D. privacy

65. From an ethical standpoint, practitioners may
   I. accept a referral fee
   II. refer a client to a single referral source
   III. use a place of employment, such as a social services agency, to recruit clients for their own private practice
   IV. refer clients only if their problems fall outside the practitioner's area of competence

   A. I and II
   B. II only
   C. II, III and IV
   D. I, II, III and IV

66. According to Carol H. Meyer's widely used model of social work assessment, the first step in the assessment process is

   A. evaluation
   B. inferential thinking
   C. problem definition
   D. exploration

67. What is the term for the theory that explains how people generate explanations for the behaviors of others?

   A. Attribution theory
   B. Stereotyping

C. Thematic apperception
D. Implicit personality theory

68. The most important professional risk associated with amalgamating groups under very broad headings or labels, such as "Asian American," is that

    A. these terms are considered derogatory by many people
    B. most immigrants to this country proudly insist on being referred to as simply "American"
    C. many people resent being folded in to a larger group for the purpose of classification
    D. the label may obscure significant differences in the culture and experiences of individuals or subgroups within the larger category

69. Before entering a social work field placement program, prospective students are ethically entitled to know
    I. dismissal policies and procedures
    II. employment prospects for graduates
    III. the basis for performance evaluation
    IV. names and theoretical perspectives of prospective supervisors

    A. I only
    B. I, II, and III
    C. III only
    D. I, II, III and IV

70. Of the steps involved in recruitment and training at human services organizations, the FIRST typically involves

    A. reference and background checks
    B. posting position announcements
    C. screening interviews
    D. developing a job description

71. During an intake interview, a client generally avoids making eye contact with the practitioner. Averting the eyes in this way is an example of the _____ function of eye contact.

    A. monitoring
    B. expressive
    C. regulatory
    D. cognitive

72. The educational success of American children and youth is highly correlated to

    A. home schooling
    B. regional employment patterns
    C. family values
    D. race and ethnicity

73. Which of the following techniques is a client-centered practitioner MOST likely to use?

    A. Response shaping
    B. Reflection

C. Giving advice
D. Analysis

74. During a meeting with a client who has just ended his marriage after twelve years, the client insists repeatedly that everything is fine. No matter what the practitioner asks or tries to suggest, the response is the same. The client is engaging in the facial management technique known as

A. neutralizing
B. masking
C. intensifying
D. deintensifying

75. A practitioner is considering a dual relationship with a client. Before forming such a relationship, the practitioner should consider
   I. divergent responsibilities
   II. incompatible expectations
   III. the power differential
   IV. referring the client to another practitioner

A. I and II
B. I, II and III
C. II, III and IV
D. I, II, III and IV

KEY (CORRECT ANSWERS)

1.	A	16.	B	31.	A	46.	B	61.	B
2.	C	17.	B	32.	D	47.	C	62.	B
3.	C	18.	B	33.	B	48.	B	63.	A
4.	D	19.	C	34.	B	49.	A	64.	D
5.	D	20.	A	35.	A	50.	B	65.	B
6.	C	21.	A	36.	B	51.	A	66.	D
7.	B	22.	A	37.	A	52.	A	67.	A
8.	B	23.	A	38.	A	53.	C	68.	D
9.	C	24.	C	39.	C	54.	C	69.	B
10.	B	25.	C	40.	C	55.	D	70.	D
11.	D	26.	B	41.	A	56.	D	71.	C
12.	A	27.	D	42.	C	57.	C	72.	D
13.	C	28.	A	43.	C	58.	C	73.	B
14.	B	29.	B	44.	B	59.	A	74.	A
15.	A	30.	D	45.	B	60.	C	75.	B

108

EXAMINATION SECTION
TEST 1

DIRECTIONS: Each question or incomplete statement is followed by several suggested answers or completions. Select the one that BEST answers the question or completes the statement. *PRINT THE LETTER OF THE CORRECT ANSWER IN THE SPACE AT THE RIGHT.*

1. For children, divorce has been identified as a risk factor for
    I. being abused
    II. substance abuse
    III. lower academic achievement
    IV. criminal involvement

    A. I and II
    B. II and III
    C. II, III and IV
    D. I, II, III and IV

2. In formulating useful goals with clients, a social worker is guided by several principles. Which of the following is NOT one of these principles?

    A. Goal formulation is often delimited by the purpose of the agency, and may necessitate referral.
    B. It is necessary to designate a target person whose condition is to be changed or maintained.
    C. Goals should always be stated positively in terms of *doing* something, rather than simply *not doing* something.
    D. The establishment of a time frame for achievement is counterproductive in the formulation of goals.

3. In selecting members for group social work, homogeneity will prove most important regarding

    A. intelligence
    B. ethnicity
    C. age, especially for young children
    D. common interests

4. A practitioner will probably NOT work well with diverse populations if he

    A. believes he is free from any racist attitudes, beliefs, or feelings
    B. is comfortable with the differences between himself and clients
    C. is flexible in applying theories to specific situations
    D. is open to being challenged and teste

5. "Non-verbal" messages of practitioners and clients refer to

    A. statements that nobody should be permitted to make in an interpersonal relationship
    B. ideas and thoughts that are left unrevealed

C. written or otherwise documented statements about problems, recommendations, and solutions
D. the entire range of facial and body expressions that communicate feelings

6. During an assessment interview, a social worker should usually avoid asking _____ questions.

   A. "why"
   B. probing
   C. open-ended
   D. closed-ended

7. Common goals of foster parent organizations include each of the following, EXCEPT

   A. elevating the public's regard for foster care
   B. the facilitation of adoption by foster parents
   C. influencing legislation that concerns children and natural parents
   D. disseminating information among foster parents

8. "Homeostasis" is a concept that has been traditionally used to describe how

   A. organisms maintain a constant external environment
   B. organisms keep themselves stable through self-regulating mechanisms
   C. humans tend to form groups or tribes around food supplies
   D. humans display a broad but fixed range of behaviors

9. A practitioner welcomes a client at the door of his office by saying, "Come in and sit down." He gestures to the room and the chair inside. This gesture is a _____ of the practitioner's verbal message

   A. complementation
   B. repetition
   C. regulation
   D. contradiction

10. In interviewing clients, practitioners should be careful to avoid nonverbal behaviors that are generally considered to be negative. These gestures include each of the following, EXCEPT

    A. body rotated slightly away from the client
    B. crossing and recrossing legs
    C. slightly backward body lean
    D. frequent eye contact

11. A practitioner asks himself: "Is our agency's program doing what it had hoped to do?" He is asking himself a _____ question.

    A. client outcome assessment
    B. intervention effectiveness
    C. process evaluation
    D. program evaluation

12. Of the following, which provides the BEST definition of the process of social work?

A. A distinct set of skills that allow the worker to tap into a variety of skills to improve conditions surrounding the client system
B. A helping activity undertaken to improve social functioning through direct involvement with the client or the systems that impact him
C. A series of programmed interventions designed to shape the client and his environment
D. A professional service to people in need who are unwilling or unable to act in their own best interests

13. Which of the following is NOT a basic component of social work "competence," as defined by the NASW?

   A. Accepting responsibility or employment only on the basis of existing competence or the intention to acquire the necessary competence.
   B. Not allowing their personal problems, psychosocial distress, legal problems, substance abuse, or mental health difficulties to interfere with professional judgment and performance.
   C. Basing practice on recognized knowledge, including empirically based knowledge, relevant to social work and social work ethics.
   D. Striving to become and remain proficient in professional practice and the performance of professional functions.

14. For practitioners who hope to draw upon Piaget's theory of cognitive development in their work with clients, probably the biggest shortcoming of his theory is that it

   A. does not examine any cognitive development beyond adolescence
   B. pigeonholes clients into distinct categories
   C. excludes questions of morality
   D. does not examine behavioral components of cognitions

15. Which of the following is true of institutional discrimination?

   A. It is often concealed through legal maneuverings.
   B. It is limited to large, formal organizations.
   C. It is woven into the fabric of society.
   D. It is a construction of the elite.

16. In the solution-focused model of intervention, the best way to solve problems is to

   A. discover when the client is not having a problem, and then build on that
   B. understand the goals and ambitions of the client
   C. determine the function that the problematic behavior serves for the client
   D. define the problem in terms of the client's external environment

17. A child in Piaget's preoperational stage
   I. is capable of altruism
   II. uses transductive reasoning
   III. is egocentric
   IV. derives thought from sensation and movement

   A. I and II
   B. I, III and IV

C. II and III
D. I, II, III and IV

18. Which of the following is NOT a primary human motive?

    A. Desire for competence
    B. Avoidance of pain
    C. Thirst
    D. Hunger

19. Summarizing clients' statements is an active listening strategy that is often useful for distilling statements into their important elements. The FIRST step in developing a good summarization of client statements during an interview is to

    A. covertly restating the message or series of messages to yourself
    B. listening for the presence of "feeling" words
    C. ask the client to summarize for herself
    D. identify any relevant patterns themes, or multiple elements

20. Each of the following is considered to be a desirable outcome of an initial interview with an applicant for social services, EXCEPT that the applicant

    A. leaves confident of working with the practitioner or case manager toward a satisfactory solution
    B. understands his/her responsibilities in the treatment or intervention
    C. feels free to express him/herself
    D. feeling some rapport with the practitioner or case manager

21. When counseling clients, social work practitioners will generally be effective if they
    I. are able to recognize and accept their own power
    II. can focus on the present moment
    III. remain in the active process of developing their own counseling style
    IV. are not afraid to offer advice

    A. I and III
    B. I, II and III
    C. II, III and IV
    D. I, II, III and IV

22. According to the NASW's code of ethics, social workers who have direct knowledge of a social work colleague's incompetence should FIRST

    A. consult with that colleague when feasible and assist the colleague in taking remedial action
    B. take action through the appropriate channels established by the employers or agency
    C. notify the NASW and any appropriate licensing and regulating bodies
    D. solicit the opinion of at least one other social worker with approximately equal qualifications and responsibilities to determine a course of action

23. Countertransference, if recognized by the practitioner, can be a useful element in a client relationship. Often, however, it is not helpful or even hurtful. Hurtful forms typically involve each of the following, EXCEPT countertransference that

A. causes a practitioner to emit subtle clues that "lead" the client
B. causes a practitioner to adopt the role the client wants us to play in his or her traditional "script"
C. is used at a distance to generate empathy for the client
D. blinds a practitioner from an important area of exploration

24. During any intervention, a social worker's final activities are aimed at _____ in the client's everyday functioning.
    I. stabilizing success
    II. generalizing outcomes
    III. preventing recidivism
    IV. restricting options

    A. I and II
    B. I and III
    C. II, III and IV
    D. I, II, III and IV

25. In the documentation and report writing phase of assessment, a service coordinator's documentation responsibilities usually consist of

    A. social histories and intake summaries
    B. medical and social histories
    C. staff notes and mental status examinations
    D. intake summaries and staff notes

26. A social work practitioner is MOST likely to increase the chances of his clients' connecting with the appropriate services when he

    A. refers clients to other more skilled professionals in the hope that these professionals will be able to determine how best to meet the clients' needs
    B. promotes self determination by providing a list of agencies in the area and allowing the clients to decide who can best meet their needs
    C. acquire expertise in as many areas of social work practice as possible, in order to directly provide needed services
    D. becomes knowledgeable about programs and providers available, and actively brokers needed services

27. One explanation for the steady increase in the divorce rate in the United States is that industrialization and urbanization led to a change in the roles played by family members. This explanation is consistent with the _____ perspective.

    A. symbolic interaction
    B. structural functionalist
    C. subcultural
    D. social conflict

28. One of the most significant criticisms about the use of strategic planning in human services organizations is that it

    A. leaves many stakeholders in the dark about the organization's objectives
    B. limits responsiveness to changing community needs

C. erodes employee morale and commitment to the organizational mission
D. is often too abstract to be useful in day-to-day management

29. The way in which a practitioner conceptualizes a client's problem configuration is known as

    A. conceptualization
    B. the internal working model
    C. mental set
    D. framing

30. Significant factors that have contributed to the changing nature of American families since the 1970s include
    I. an increase in births outside marriage
    II. a greater number of remarriages in which partners bring children from previous relationships
    III. altered gender role expectations
    IV. an increase in the number of partners who divorce or separate

    A. I, II and IV
    B. I and III
    C. III only
    D. I, II, III and IV

31. Culture maintains boundaries in each of the following ways, EXCEPT by

    A. instilling a sense of genuineness about the alternatives peculiar to a society
    B. constructing symbols and meanings
    C. limiting the ranges of acceptable behavior and attitudes
    D. establishing the tendency for people to think of other societies as inferior

32. The solution-focused perspective defines a client who describes a problem but isn't willing to work on solving it as a

    A. resistor
    B. complainant
    C. dam-builder
    D. procrastinator

33. During an assessment interview, a practitioner is trying to identify the range of problems that a client is experiencing. Which of the following communication skills is most appropriately used for this purpose?

    A. Open-ended questions
    B. Closed-ended questions
    C. Confrontation
    D. Interpretation

34. Social workers who have unresolved personal conflicts should

    A. recognize that their problems may interfere with the effectiveness and avoid activities or responses that could harm a client
    B. repress any anxiety-provoking issues in their own lives before attempting to work with others

C. use their experience to lead clients in a mutual resolution of these problems
D. resolve these conflicts before planning a client interventionand ideally, before meeting the client at all.

35. Based largely on the understanding that all people break rules at one time or another, _____ theorists make the assumption that what we call "deviant" is actually part of an overall pattern of normality.

    A. labeling
    B. social Darwinism
    C. conflict
    D. order

36. Rural clients tend to evaluate social workers on the basis of

    A. the level of education the worker has achieved
    B. help delivered or problems solved
    C. the type of intervention used
    D. areas of specialization

37. A client is having trouble at work. He tells the practitioner "I have a hard time relating to authority figures." He is describing his problem behavior

    A. in a way that places responsibility squarely on himself
    B. covertly
    C. in nonbehavioral terms
    D. without any affective cues

38. The practice of limiting a client's right to self-determination in order to protect him or her from self-harm is known in social work as

    A. gatekeeping
    B. paternalism
    C. delimiting behavior
    D. proxy

39. Which of the following is LEAST likely to be a symptom of stress?

    A. Emotional instability
    B. Lethargy
    C. Sleep problems
    D. Digestive problems

40. In the traditional clinical model of school social work, a practitioner was probably LEAST likely to execute the role of

    A. enabler
    B. consultant
    C. supporter
    D. advocate

41. When advocating for a client, the first attempt at advocacy should always be

    A. a legal challenge
    B. a formal appeal
    C. temperate persuasion
    D. widely spread publicity about the client's case

42. During regular meetings with his practitioner, a client has the tendency to ascribe the achievements of others to good luck or easy tasks, while assuming his failures to be due to a lack of ability or experience. The client's thinking is a phenomenon known as

    A. fundamental attribution bias
    B. the Hawthorne effect
    C. self-serving bias
    D. the halo effect

43. The responsibilities of social work intern instructors typically include each of the following, EXCEPT

    A. clearly stating roles and responsibilities of interns in the field
    B. clearly stating the roles and responsibilities of site supervisors
    C. acting on site supervisors' recommendations following a negative intern evaluation
    D. developing clear field placement policies

44. A teenage client has been having problems in school he is constantly being disciplined for being disruptive. Discussions with the client reveal that even though he has lost several privileges at school, he is reluctant to give up his disruptive behavior because of the attention it brings in from his peers. The attention of the client's peers is an example of a(n)

    A. secondary gain
    B. behavioral consequence
    C. negative reinforcement
    D. cognitive dissonance

45. Which of the following is NOT a typical purpose of client self-monitoring?

    A. To shift the burden of decision-making onto the client
    B. To validate the accuracy of the client's reports during interviews
    C. To test out hunches about the problem.
    D. To help practitioner and client gain information about what actually occurs with respect to the problem in real-life situations

46. Which of the following is a "lower-order" human need, as identified in Maslow's hierarchy?

    A. Belonging
    B. Status
    C. Fulfillment
    D. Security

47. Gene, a social worker, finds himself wanting to solve his client's problems with alcohol dependency, which are similar to problems Gene's own son went through several years ago. Gene gives advice and is frustrated when the client doesn't follow through on his suggestions. Gene's emotional reactions to his client are based on

    A. countertransference
    B. nurturing
    C. transference
    D. empathy

48. In the termination phase of treatment, strategies for maintaining client gains may include each of the following, EXCEPT

    A. increasing the client's sense of mastery through realistic praise
    B. anticipating and planning for possible future difficulties
    C. highlighting and specifying the client's role in maintaining change
    D. teaching the client to deal with problems that underlie a coping pattern

49. After receiving a notification about a 10-year-old boy's underperfor-mance at school, a social worker has tried twice to arrange a meeting with the boy's 28-year-old mother, who works long hours as a waitress and has sole responsibility for his care. Both times, the mother has cancelled the meeting at the last minute, citing sudden work conflicts.
The social worker schedules an in-home visit to the boy's familybut when he arrives, he is told by the boy that the mother is at work. The child's grandmother also lives in the home, but is bedridden, and the boy and his sister help care for her. The family's apartment is in disarray, with dirty dishes stacked in the sink and on the stovetop. Laundry is strewn about in wrinkled piles. The social worker observes no alcohol in the house, and the grandmother, who is cooperative, says that her daughter doesn't drink, and never has.
As the social worker continues to monitor this family, he should be especially alert for signs of

    A. a personality disorder on the part of the mother
    B. child abuse
    C. substance abuse
    D. child neglect

50. Within practice settings that call upon the practitioner's knowledge and skill at all levels of the organization, the social work profession is considered to be a(n) _____ discipline.

    A. primary
    B. secondary
    C. collegial
    D. ancillary

51. Among gays and lesbians, stress and a lack of emotional support have been shown to contribute to

    A. high rates of alcoholism
    B. promiscuity
    C. identity fragmentation
    D. erratic employment patterns

52. An elderly client is particularly concerned about being "bothered" all the time by a social work practitioner who frequently visits her home. To avoid too much discomfort on the part of the client, the practitioner has the client sign several blank consent forms so that her medical history can be sent to several agencies that might offer supportive services. In this case, the worker has

   A. violated the principle of informed consent
   B. hit upon a key strategy for avoiding burnout
   C. demonstrated ignorance of the eligibility rules for most service agencies
   D. found an ethical strategy for streamlining an often frustrating bureaucracy

53. The most common diagnoses for people who complete suicide are

   A. schizophrenia and substance abuse
   B. depressive illness and borderline personality disorder
   C. depressive illness and alcoholism
   D. schizophrenia and chronic metabolic disease

54. The mother of a 14-year-old girl telephoned crisis services, telling the worker that her son had just locked and barricaded himself in his room. Earlier, she had overheard a conversation between the boy and his girlfriend that was clearly a fight. She is concerned because the boy had tried to overdose after the end of an earlier relationship.
A worker was immediately dispatched to the residence. After a lengthy conversation in which the worker successfully established rapport with the boy, the boy agreed to let the worker in.
Thus far, crisis services and the worker have followed the formula of Roberts' Seven-Stage Crisis Intervention Model. As a next step, the worker will attempt to

   A. explore alternatives to suicide, such as inpatient or outpatient services
   B. identify and validate the boy's emotions
   C. develop an action plan with the boy
   D. have the boy identify what he views as the major problem or problems

55. The primary goal of crisis intervention can best be described as

   A. protecting the client from a situation in which he or she has become more likely to experience a traumatic event than other people
   B. helping the client to identify and endure the long-term consequences of a traumatic event
   C. protecting a client from self-harm following a traumatic event
   D. helping the client to identify and cope with the sense of "disequilibrium" in the aftermath of a trauma

56. A practitioner discovers that a client is behaving in a way that is seriously damaging both to himself and a close relative. While respecting the concept of self-determination and confidentiality, the practitioner should

   A. warn the client that he (the practitioner) has an obligation to divulge the client's behavior to the appropriate agency or authority, and then do so
   B. attempt to dissuade the client from further engaging in behavior that is harmful
   C. immediately alert the authorities
   D. refer the client to a social services worker who has more experience in this specific type of behavior

57. In order to serve effectively in rural communities, social work practitioners would most likely need to incorporate the concepts of _____ into their practice.

    A. nature and seasonal fluctuation
    B. self-reliance and mutual aid
    C. land and ownership
    D. religion and spirituality

58. Which of the following is NOT typically included in a service agreement between a practitioner and a client?

    A. Description of the agency's programs and services
    B. Fees for service or arrangements for reimbursement
    C. Theoretical framework for the relationship
    D. Time frames for the provision of services

59. From a legal perspective, case records

    A. belong to the practitioner who created them
    B. belong to the client
    C. belong to the agency at which they are physically held
    D. are for the benefit of the client

60. A practitioner is speaking to a client via cellular phone. The practitioner should be aware that
    I. there is a chance that the call could be intercepted by an unauthorized party
    II. the client may not be in a private place
    III. telephone conversations are not considered to be a public service
    IV. complete privacy cannot be assured

    A. I and II
    B. I, II, and IV
    C. III only
    D. I, II, III and IV

61. The basic assumptions underlying social work administration do NOT include the statement that

    A. each person who works within the agency should be considered a stakeholder in agency outcomes
    B. administration is largely the process of securing and transforming community resources
    C. the major contributions toward the improvement of administration come from management itself
    D. the agency has the primary responsibility for the creation and control of its own destiny

62. Most Asian Americans who are seeking from a social work practitioner are looking for a professional who is

    A. nondirective
    B. problem-focused
    C. goal-oriented
    D. experiential in focus

63. Privileged communication is NOT

   A. widely varying in state-to-state legal definitions
   B. usually waived if a third party is present
   C. particularly difficult to protect when working with married couples
   D. protected no matter what the risks involved

64. In devising a treatment plan, a practitioner begins with client tasks that can be managed fairly easily and with some success, before moving on to the larger issues that are causing problems. In doing so, the practitioner is adhering to the rule of

   A. successive approximations
   B. object orientation
   C. positive reinforcement
   D. mental set

65. "Preparatory empathy" is a process that is used by a practitioner in order to

   A. insure against client deception
   B. streamline an intervention by figuring some things out in advance
   C. choose necessary resources or services
   D. make him more aware of issues or barriers that might be encountered

66. The federal WIC program specifically targets the health and welfare of

   A. abused children
   B. adoptive families
   C. pregnant women and newborn children
   D. unskilled laborers who have been injured on the job

67. Of all Hispanics living the United States, those of Mexican descent account for about _____ percent of the total.

   A. 20
   B. 40
   C. 60
   D. 80

68. From her first few meetings with a client, a social work practitioner has begun to form an impression. If the practitioner seeks out additional information that will help to confirm or deny her existing impressions, she will be engaging in

   A. cognitive integration
   B. active perception
   C. offensive perception
   D. thematic apperception

69. A social worker is using the person-in-environment (PIE) system of client assessment. In describing the environmental problems that affect a client's social functioning, the social worker will rely on six groupings of social system problems. Which of the following is NOT one of the groupings used in the PIE system?

   A. Economic/basic need
   B. Judicial/legal system

C. Physical health
D. Education and training

70. Basic social work values that influence professional practice include each of the following, EXCEPT   70.____

    A. self-determination
    B. the inherent uniqueness of a person
    C. individualism
    D. the inherent worth and dignity of a person

71. Which step in the listening process involves the assignment of meaning to a message?   71.____

    A. Encoding
    B. Attending
    C. Understanding
    D. Selecting

72. Qualitative social work research   72.____

    A. observes people in natural settings and focuses on the meaning they assign to experiences.
    B. is analyzed through the use of bivariate methods
    C. details the past in order to understand present conditions
    D. compares statistics from number of cases

73. When a worker attempts to "cement" a referral, she is attempting to   73.____

    A. make sure the client is connected to the suggested resource
    B. make the working relationship into a strong enough bond that the client will be sure to follow through
    C. use software or another evaluative tool that confirms the appropriateness of the client to the proposed resource
    D. suggest to the client in advance that the referral will result in success

74. In working with a client, a practitioner is careful to avoid singling out one or two obvious client characteristics as the reason for everything the person does. The tendency to do this is known as   74.____

    A. stereotyping
    B. scripting
    C. over-attribution
    D. highballing

75. A group's sense of ethnic identity is affected by the
    I. degree to which the members' physical appearances differ from those in mainstream society
    II. size of the group
    III. amount of power the group has
    IV. extent of assimilation

    A. I only
    B. I and III
    C. II and IV
    D. I, II, III and IV

KEY (CORRECT ANSWERS)

1. D	16. A	31. A	46. D	61. C
2. D	17. C	32. B	47. A	62. A
3. C	18. A	33. A	48. D	63. D
4. A	19. A	34. A	49. D	64. A
5. D	20. B	35. A	50. A	65. D
6. A	21. B	36. B	51. A	66. C
7. B	22. A	37. C	52. A	67. C
8. B	23. C	38. B	53. C	68. B
9. B	24. A	39. B	54. D	69. C
10. D	25. D	40. D	55. D	70. C
11. D	26. D	41. C	56. A	71. C
12. B	27. B	42. A	57. B	72. A
13. A	28. D	43. C	58. C	73. A
14. A	29. A	44. A	59. B	74. C
15. C	30. D	45. A	60. B	75. D

TEST 2

DIRECTIONS: Each question or incomplete statement is followed by several suggested answers or completions. Select the one that BEST answers the question or completes the statement. *PRINT THE LETTER OF THE CORRECT ANSWER IN THE SPACE AT THE RIGHT.*

1. In the _____ style of conflict management, the parties attempt to separate themselves from the problem.

    A. cooperative
    B. nonconfrontational
    C. mediative
    D. settlement

2. The purposes of staff notes, or progress notes, include
    I. recording client's responses to services
    II. connecting a service to a key issue
    III. describing client status
    IV. providing direction for ongoing treatment

    A. I only
    B. I, II and III
    C. III and IV
    D. I, II, III and IV

3. A genogram is an assessment tool that

    A. involves DNA sampling
    B. defers consideration of current family relationships
    C. gives a picture of family relationships over at least three generations
    D. uses statistical measures to calculate the probability of an intervention's success

4. Which of the following is NOT a belief of stage theorists?

    A. The progression of stages is biologically programmed.
    B. Children pass through the same stages in the same sequence.
    C. Stages are usually marked by age ranges.
    D. As children progress through the stages, the differences between them are quantitative.

5. During the opening phase of a client interview, the practitioner should probably spend most of his time and thoughts on

    A. self-disclosure
    B. negotiating a working contract
    C. interpreting behaviors
    D. explaining agency rules and protocols

6. Behaviors commonly associated with substance abuse include
    I. a withdrawal from responsibility
    II. unusual outbreaks of temper
    III. abrupt changes in quality or output of work
    IV. wearing sunglasses at inappropriate times

A. I and II
B. I, II and III
C. II and IV
D. I, II, III and IV

7. Which of the following would a practitioner typically do FIRST in a problem assessment interview?

    A. Identify client coping skills
    B. Identify the range of client problems
    C. Prioritize and select issues and problems for discussion
    D. Identify consequences of problem behaviors

8. A social worker's primary ethical duty is to

    A. effect social justice
    B. promote the welfare of the client
    C. respect diversity
    D. avoid dependent relationships

9. The person-centered model of human behavior views the major reason for maladjustment as a(n)

    A. failure to set a self-actualizing tendency in motion
    B. inability to establish unconditional positive regard
    C. incongruence between self-concept and experience
    D. unresolved childhood frustrations

10. The person-in-environment (PIE) system of client assessment is a four-factor system. Factor _____ provides a statement of the client's physical health problems.

    A. I
    B. II
    C. III
    D. IV

11. An adolescent client tells her social worker that she feels she is the only person in the world who has ever had such strong unrequited love for another person—the boy who sits next to her in geometry class. The component of adolescent egocentrism being enacted by the girl is the

    A. all-or-none fallacy
    B. imaginary audience
    C. questionable cause
    D. personal fable

12. Research into interpersonal relationships suggests that women often build relationships through shared positive feelings, while men often build relationships through

    A. shared activities
    B. shared opinions
    C. metacommunication
    D. impression management

13. Which of the following is NOT typically a purpose of assessment? 13._____

    A. To identify the controlling or contributing variables associated with a client's problem
    B. To launch the first phase of treatment
    C. To educate and motivate the client by sharing views about the problem
    D. To plan effective interventions and strategies

14. Persuading clients to abandon mistaken ways of thinking is a goal of 14._____

    A. client-centered therapy
    B. operant conditioning
    C. cognitive therapy
    D. systematic desensitization

15. A practitioner is creating an action plan with an adult client who has decided to leave his current job. Typically, planning such a move requires practitioner and client to move on to 15._____

    A. ensure that the work to be done fits an accepted model of treatment
    B. breaking large goals into component parts
    C. making the client aware of the full range of consequences
    D. ensure that this decision meets with the approval of the people who will be affected by it

16. Some of the information in an applicant's file comes from secondary sources. Which of the following is NOT considered a secondary source? 16._____

    A. Applicant's family
    B. Referring agency
    C. School
    D. Current staff notes

17. Self-disclosure is considered a "discretionary" response in discussions with clients, because it 17._____

    A. is not considered to be therapeutic
    B. is only used if the client requests it
    C. should be used carefully to avoid taking the focus off the client
    D. requires a familiarity with the client's worldview before it is used

18. For a practitioner working from the family systems theory, symptoms of maladjustment in families are usually masked by 18._____

    A. the involvement and recommendations of professionals who were previously involved
    B. the presenting crisis or problem that initially brought the family into contact with the agency
    C. abusive relationships
    D. environmental components in the family's community

19. A school social worker is told that one of the kindergartners is running around, out of control, and disrupting the others at naptime. As she attempts to understand the problem, her FIRST step should be to 19._____

A. arrange an interview with the school psychologist
B. look into finding an alternative school placement
C. systematically observe the child in the classroom to see how it is managed
D. contact the parents to inform them of the child's behavior problems

20. What is the collective term applied to communication variables such as voice level, pitch, rate, and fluency of speech?

    A. Kinesics
    B. Paralinguistics
    C. Nonverbal messages
    D. Proxemics

21. Although the terms *counseling* and *interviewing* are sometimes used interchangeably in social work, there are differences that should be noted. Which of the following is NOT one of these differences.

    A. Interviewing is a responsibility that can be assumed by most practitioners or case managers.
    B. Interviewing is a more basic process for information gathering and problem solving.
    C. Counseling is a more intensive and personal process.
    D. Counseling is often associated with nonprofessional workers, whereas therapy used to indicate professional interventions.

22. A social worker in the _____ role is conducting "macro" practice.
    I. manager
    II. planner
    III. case manager
    IV. mediator

    A. I and II
    B. I, II and IV
    C. III only
    D. I, II, III and IV

23. The final stage of Elisabeth Kubler-Ross's theory of how people handle the knowledge of their impending death is known as

    A. denial
    B. bargaining
    C. anger
    D. acceptance

24. Probably the most important factor in establishing a working alliance with a client is the

    A. client's belief about whether the practitioner attends and understands
    B. accuracy of the practitioner's assessment of the presenting problem(s)
    C. practitioner's effort to be empathetic
    D. client's initial willingness to change

25. During the assessment phase, the practice of _____ means that the practitioner and client are setting specific objectives.

   A. activating resources
   B. framing solutions
   C. defining the problem
   D. weighing alternatives

26. Reflecting and paraphrasing are two active listening strategies often used by practitioners to help clients become more aware of the implications of their own statements. Basically the difference between reflecting and paraphrasing involves the difference between the

   A. client's words and the client's actions
   B. the emotional (affective) and factual (cognitive) content of messages
   C. way the client perceives the world and the way the world actually is
   D. way the client is expressing a message and the way it is being received by the practitioner

27. The process by which people shape social life by adapting to, negotiating with, and changing social structures is known as

   A. determinism
   B. positivism
   C. human agency
   D. ideology

28. Child welfare is a social work practice area that

   A. focuses on issues, problems, and policies related to the well-being of children
   B. administers school lunches and other benefit programs for low-income children
   C. focuses on increasing the educational potential of children
   D. mainly works to broker adoptions

29. The relationship between social work supervisors and supervisees, which parallels the relationship between social worker and client, has been described in terms of basic relational elements. Which of the following is NOT one of these?

   A. Caring
   B. Rapport
   C. Authority
   D. Trust

30. The _____ model attributes the essential characteristics of consensus, cohesion, stability, reciprocity, and cooperation to society.

   A. evolutionary
   B. conflict
   C. order
   D. symbolic interaction

31. Upholding rules, regulations and restrictions of a social services agency which are not always best for the client is a function of the social worker's role known as

    A. gatekeeping
    B. spoilage
    C. advocacy
    D. bureaucratic blindness

32. A social worker and her client have developed a long-range goal. Now they are determining individual steps that will lead to the achievement of that goal. This is a process known as

    A. chunking
    B. prioritizing
    C. partializing
    D. contracting

33. Community surveys, policy analyses, and case histories are examples of

    A. social studies
    B. ecomaps
    C. needs assessments
    D. genograms

34. In a social services agency that serves teenage runaways, an example of a direct service strategy would be

    A. organizing
    B. counseling
    C. gathering information
    D. planning

35. Compared to others in society, those with superior _____ are more likely to support the status quo.

    A. educational achievement
    B. social locations
    C. value systems
    D. incomes

36. "Primary prevention" means

    A. the severity and duration of a disease or disorder have been reduced
    B. clinical means have been used to provide treatment, such as crisis intervention
    C. a disease or disorder is stopped at its source, and the cause is eliminated
    D. the spread of a disease or disorder among people has been limited

37. Under normal circumstances it is considered acceptable practice for a social worker to disclose a client's confidential information to
    I. the practitioner's supervisor as it relates to the supervisory relationship
    II. professionals who are consulted about assessments or interventions
    III. third-party payers for the purpose of justifying treatment decisions
    IV. close family members for the purpose of developing understanding of the client's particular difficulties

A. I only
B. I and II
C. I, II and III
D. I, II, III and IV

38. A client's feelings of powerlessness can be reduced when a social worker adopts each of the following roles, EXCEPT the role of

   A. resource consultant, who connects the client to goods and services
   B. advocate, who acts as the client's protector in social living matters
   C. sensitizer, who helps the client gain knowledge needed to solve problems
   D. educator, who facilitates the learning and skill development needed for goal setting and task completion

38.____

39. The _____ model of human services organization management places the greatest value on maximizing the productivity of the organization.

   A. internal process
   B. open-system
   C. rational goal
   D. human relations

39.____

40. During an interview, practitioner and client establish a goal for the client to use her time more efficiently at work and at home. This is an example of a _____ goal.

   A. process
   B. survival
   C. treatment
   D. service

40.____

41. One reason people often confuse race and ethnicity is because they

   A. are suspicious of people who are different from themselves
   B. are unaware that race is cultural and ethnicity is biological
   C. see cultural differences and define race in specific, often inaccurate ways
   D. have met few people outside their own race

41.____

42. Dual relationships between a practitioner and a client, according to the NASW:

   A. should not be formed if there is any possibility for exploitation or potential harm to the client
   B. are usually an unavoidable part of professional practice
   C. are generally acceptable if social workers take steps to protect clients
   D. are generally acceptable if social workers are careful to avoid legal problems that could damage the status of the social work profession

42.____

43. In a family intervention that implements the structural model, the family will be expected to

   A. submit to the direction of the practitioner
   B. solve their own problems
   C. shift their internal alliances
   D. shift blame to the external environment

43.____

44. In diversion programs, social workers typically provide

   A. case management services with probation officers in an attempt to prevent recidivism
   B. consultation services about early-release programs for juvenile offenders
   C. counseling services through a network of lay professionals
   D. crisis intervention or referral services aimed at avoiding imprisonment

45. In hospital social work, an example of macropractice would be

   A. connecting with community providers to maintain understanding of community needs
   B. increasing health provider awareness of clients' home environment
   C. engaging clients in planning for their immediate future after discharge
   D. educating clients and families about the implications of a particular illness or disorder

46. A client tells a practitioner that he is distraught over the end of his marriage and wishes he could "just go to sleep forever, be at peace, and not have to feel this pain any more." The practitioner should

   A. assess whether the client is suicidal and intervene if necessary
   B. recognize that such statements are often merely a "cry for help" and urge the client to focus on more practical issues
   C. contact the client's wife and determine whether there is a chance to reconcile
   D. immediately commit the client to a psychiatric facility

47. The presenting problems of most African American clients are rooted in

   A. genetics
   B. personality deficits
   C. stress from external systems
   D. unresolved family conflicts

48. A solution-focused intervention would most likely involve the goal of

   A. a first-order change in the client system
   B. behavioral continuity
   C. a perceptual shift from talking about problems to talking about how to solve them
   D. determining exactly how a problem came into being

49. During an interview in which a client is being evaluated, the client should understand that the

   A. information gained during the interview may be the basis of a report on the client
   B. questions will not be upsetting to him/her
   C. interview will focus on the client's well-being
   D. he or she has implicitly entered into a service contract

50. The _____ theory of rural social work asserts that there are distinct differences between rural and urban areas, and that the urban end of the continuum is associated with social pathology.

A. classical
B. subcultural
C. compositional
D. determinist

51. During the supervisory discussion of a client case, the FIRST topic of discussion should typically be

    A. client dynamics and problems
    B. alternative intervention strategies
    C. a tentative assessment or diagnosis
    D. selection of a general treatment approach

52. The millions of Asian Americans living in the United States today represent a generally _____ population.

    A. prosperous
    B. culturally homogeneous
    C. mainstreamed
    D. heterogeneous

53. Most legal issues encountered by social work practitioners involve

    A. complaints of improper conduct
    B. being sued for negligence or malpractice
    C. being prosecuted for crimes
    D. acting as witnesses in litigation

54. The initial recommended response to a client who is suicidal is

    A. hospitalization and observation
    B. identifying the client's level of seriousness
    C. problem-solving training
    D. crisis intervention and a functional assessment of the suicidal behavior

55. The most common client reactions to the termination of direct social service include each of the following, EXCEPT

    A. pride
    B. ambivalence
    C. satisfaction
    D. denial

56. Most referrals to human service professionals are made by

    A. school systems
    B. health care workers
    C. the courts
    D. word of mouth from friends or family members

57. The term "handicap" refers to a(n)

    A. obstruction that prevents an interface between a disability and the environment
    B. an impairment that limits one's daily activities

C. inability to perform tasks at a level that is generally considered to be socially acceptable
D. loss of use or function of an organ or bodily system

58. When writing case notes, practitioners should always
    I. keep in mind that others may read the notes
    II. compose them immediately after a client meeting
    III. provide as much detail as possible
    IV. use shorthand

    A. I and II
    B. II only
    C. I, II and III
    D. I, II, III and

59. The most frequent cause of child death is

    A. physical abuse
    B. suicide
    C. being left unsupervised or alone for long periods of time
    D. automobile accidents

60. Clients of social service agencies often disagree with either agency policies or a practitioner's actions, or both. If a client demands to know why a particular action was taken and perhaps reverse it, he or she is exercising a right to

    A. confidentiality
    B. due process
    C. privileged information
    D. informed consent

61. Content theories of human motivation argue that

    A. most people dislike change
    B. external consequences determine behavior
    C. most people are affiliation-oriented
    D. internal needs lead to behavior

62. Once a client's service needs are clear, a social worker often helps the client choose the most appropriate service and negotiates the terms of service delivery. Here, the social worker is acting in the role of

    A. broker
    B. consultant
    C. advocate
    D. coordinator

63. When social work practitioners commit errors in working with gay, lesbian, and bisexual clients, these errors most often stem from the

    A. workers' own unconscious prejudices
    B. failure to recognize clients as homosexual, due to a lack of identifying characteristics
    C. identification of client problems as being caused by their sexuality

D. assumption that client problems are unrelated to social oppression or stigma

64. If included statistically as a form of elder abuse, self-neglect would represent about _____ percent of cases reported to state adult protective services agencies.

   A. 5-10
   B. 20-35
   C. 40-50
   D. 60-75

65. Many social workers, especially those who work in institutional settings, use the brief treatment model in their interventions. Which of the following is NOT one of the core assumptions of this model?

   A. Problems are a normal part of life and not a sign of pathology.
   B. Practitioners believe people can change, and communicate this to their clients.
   C. The purpose of treatment is to develop insight into the underlying causes of problems.
   D. Treatment makes use of what the client brings to it

66. Stan, a Native American college student, is seeking information about work programs in the urban community where he lives. When Stan asks a female practitioner at the local agency about it, the practitioner notices that he makes very little eye contact. The practitioner should recognize that Stan

   A. would be more likely to look into her eyes if she were a male
   B. is not likely to follow through with the practitioner's recommendations or referrals
   C. is likely to view direct eye contact as a lack of respect
   D. does not express much faith in the practitioner's abilities

67. The tendency of people to perceive what they expect to perceive is a phenomenon known as

   A. self-serving bias
   B. perceptual set
   C. filtration
   D. fundamental attribution bias

68. A person's satisfaction with communication is based upon a theoretical "sum total" of the positive and negative elements in a message. This sum is a phenomenon known as message

   A. validity
   B. salience
   C. solidity
   D. valence

69. Data about how long or how often a problem occurs before an intervention are known as _____ data.

   A. raw
   B. norming
   C. baseline
   D. skewed

70. In _____ social work, assessment is also known as functional analysis.

    A. narrative
    B. behavioral
    C. feminist
    D. cognitive

71. During an assessment interview, a practitioner asks a client: "How do you feel about the fact that your drinking has harmed your relationship with your daughter?" The practitioner is trying to identify _____ consequences of the client's problem.

    A. contextual
    B. affective
    C. behavioral
    D. somatic

72. For social work research to have a meaningful function, it must be applied by practitioners. One of the major reasons practitioners fail to apply the results of research is that

    A. there is no standard methodology that would make results universally applicable
    B. many studies lack relevance to day-to-day practice decisions
    C. there is still widespread theoretical bias in the design of many studies
    D. most practitioners don't conduct research themselves

73. Of the following social sciences, social work draws most of its professional expertise from

    A. psychology
    B. economics
    C. sociology
    D. anthropology

74. In her meetings with a client, a practitioner has begun to form the perception that he may be using a combination of alcohol and illegal drugs. She decides, during subsequent meetings, to engage in "direct perception checking" in order to confirm or deny this perception. This will involve

    A. paying careful attention to the client's tone of voice
    B. observing the client's behaviors to discover cues that will either confirm or deny her impressions
    C. asking the client if he has a drug or drinking problem
    D. listening more intently to the client's words and language

75. Though practitioner self-disclosure can be a useful tool for helping clients, it is most helpful when its use is carefully assessed beforehand. Generally, practitioners should AVOID making self-disclosure statements

    A. as concise as possible
    B. as a way of introducing oneself to the client
    C. in a way that will regulate the role distance between practitioner and client
    D. similar in content and mood to the client's messages

KEY (CORRECT ANSWERS)

1. A	16. D	31. A	46. A	61. D
2. D	17. C	32. C	47. C	62. A
3. C	18. B	33. A	48. C	63. B
4. D	19. C	34. B	49. A	64. C
5. B	20. B	35. B	50. A	65. C
6. D	21. D	36. C	51. A	66. C
7. C	22. A	37. B	52. D	67. B
8. B	23. D	38. B	53. D	68. D
9. C	24. A	39. C	54. D	69. C
10. D	25. B	40. C	55. D	70. B
11. D	26. B	41. C	56. D	71. B
12. A	27. C	42. A	57. A	72. B
13. B	28. A	43. B	58. C	73. A
14. C	29. C	44. D	59. C	74. B
15. B	30. C	45. A	60. B	75. B

EXAMINATION SECTION
TEST 1

DIRECTIONS: Each question or incomplete statement is followed by several suggested answers or completions. Select the one that BEST answers the question or completes the statement. *PRINT THE LETTER OF THE CORRECT ANSWER IN THE SPACE AT THE RIGHT.*

1. Which of the following is NOT one of the major variables to take into account when considering a community needs assessment? 1.____
    A. State of program development
    B. Resources available
    C. Demographics
    D. Community attitudes

2. Which of the following behaviors or patterns should be avoided as much as possible in a group work setting? 2.____
    A. Casework in the group
    B. Recontracting
    B. Dialectical process
    D. Mutual demand

3. During an assessment interview, a social worker and a client try to clarify and analyze the client's sense of self. If the worker wants to discover something about the client's sense of self-efficacy, which of the following questions is MOST appropriate? 3.____
    A. For whom do you feel responsible and obligated to help or look after?
    B. What, if anything, would you change about yourself if it were possible?
    C. To what degree are you satisfied with your home?
    D. Do you usually respond to change with anticipation and enthusiasm, or with fear?

4. During an initial session, a family confronts the father, an alcoholic client, in order to get him to acknowledge his addiction. However, the client continues to deny a problem. The MOST appropriate question or statement from the social worker at this point would be 4.____
    A. If you were to stop drinking, do you think your life would be any different?
    B. Do you want a drink right now?
    C. I think your family is on to something here.
    D. It's clear that you have a problem, and I think you should start dealing with it.

5. A social worker should assume that any client who talks about suicide is 5.____
    A. ambivalent and hoping for assistance
    B. an immediate risk
    C. clinically depressed
    D. severely emotionally disturbed

6. In comparing a normal conversation and a helping interview, which of the following statements is generally TRUE? 6.____
    A. A conversation involves no subsequent accountability.
    B. A conversation involves a clear delineation of roles.
    C. An interview involves an equal distribution of power and authority
    D. The interaction in an interview follows social expectations and norms.

7. In the newly expanded family system (the infant family), _____ becomes a major concern for parents.

    A. Triangulation
    B. boundary negotiation
    C. latent function
    D. power sharing

8. Which of the following methods of community needs assessment relies to the greatest degree on existing public records?

    A. Social indicators
    B. Field study
    C. Rates-under treatment
    D. Key informant

9. A client, abandoned by her husband six months ago, has been trying to raise three children alone. The client is angry because her welfare check hasn't come through and her landlord is demanding rent. The landlord also refuses to make repairs to a toilet that continues to leak and poses a hazard to her children. The client tells the social worker she has bought a gun and intends to use it on the landlord. The worker should

    A. advise the client that both the landlord and the police need to be made aware of this threat
    B. disregard the threat and focus on how to pay rent and get the toilet fixed
    C. acknowledge her anger and discuss alternatives, but tell her of actions that must be taken if the threat is repeated
    D. perform a citizen's arrest of the client

10. After several weeks of an intervention program, a mother has made some progress in looking for employment, but the practitioner observes that the mother's employment-seeking behaviors do not occur frequently or steadily enough to produce the desired results. Which of the following behavioral techniques is MOST appropriate for this situation?

    A. Modeling
    B. Extinction
    C. Shaping
    D. Removal from reinforcing environment

11. A worker and client who meet periodically to recall progress made by the client over the past six meetings are engaging in a kind of

    A. summative evaluation
    B. formative evaluation
    C. goal attainment scaling
    D. task achievement scaling

12. Which of the following is NOT a goal identified by the humanist perspective of individual development?

    A. To achieve a unity of experience
    B. To achieve security through relationships
    C. To find meaning in life
    D. To realize inner potentials

13. A process contract would typically be used between a social work agency and a contracting organization to   13._____

    A. fix a level of program funding
    B. specify a certain level of client satisfaction
    C. guarantee a specific measure of service volume
    D. secure facilities for a certain program

14. A social worker meets for the first time with a young single mother of three small children. The woman's problem, simply stated, is poverty. In the language of treatment planning, a "goal" for this woman would be to   14._____

    A. earn more money
    B. get enough financial assistance to provide food, clothing, and shelter
    C. obtain Aid to Families with Dependent Children (AFDC)
    D. receive food stamps

15. Which of the following is NOT a reason why public policy would be considered part of the delivery of human services?   15._____

    A. Social workers develop and use resources in direct practice.
    B. Service workers see problems firsthand and actually implement policies.
    C. Social policy is developed by public and nonpublic agencies within prescribed parameters.
    D. Public policy is made by legislative bodies.

16. In the cognitive model of human development, a child in the "intuitive" phase is learning how to   16._____

    A. differentiate between assimilation and accommodation
    B. organize objects into hierarchies of classes
    C. understand number concepts
    D. imitate symbols

17. In considering the legal issue of informed consent, it is important to consider its three main issues. Which of the following is NOT one of these?   17._____

    A. Coerciveness of the situation
    B. Client's mental competency
    C. Completeness of information
    D. Risk to client

18. Of the following techniques or strategies that can be used by a practitioner during a client interview, which is most directive in nature?   18._____

    A. Clarifying   B. Reflecting
    C. Interpretation   D. Paraphrasing

19. The parents of failure-to-thrive babies are usually described as

    A. single parents
    B. socially isolated and beset by environmental stressors
    C. middle-class parents who both work outside the home
    D. developmentally disabled and improperly schooled in parenting

20. Which of the following types of practice evaluation is probably MOST appropriate for a hospital social worker who performs discharge planning?

    A. Task-achievement scaling
    B. Goal-attainment scaling
    C. ABAB evaluation
    D. Client satisfaction questionnaire

21. In assessing the risk of child maltreatment in a family, the practitioner evaluates "parent force" factors, which include

    A. the anticipation of how the parents will react to an intervention
    B. how the parents were treated by their own parents
    C. family demographics
    D. whether the abusive parent is drunk, depressed, explosive, etc.

22. The NASW code advises social workers to inform clients of the

    A. advantages involved in following a treatment program
    B. diagnosis and prognosis in each case
    C. ethical challenges involved in managed care
    D. limits to services that are due to third-party payer requirements

23. According to Erikson's levels of psychosocial development, the basic task of the older adult is

    A. intimacy
    B. industry
    C. ego integrity
    D. autonomy

24. The primary purpose of applying a generalist perspective to social work practice is to ensure that a worker

    A. is attentive to cultural and ethnic diversity among clients
    B. focuses on client strengths during assessment and intervention
    C. works to improve the social functioning of individuals, couples, or families
    D. approaches every client and situation in a way that is open to the use of various models, theories, and techniques

25. Which of the following is NOT typically an objective of mobilization?

    A. To convince existing community resources to alter their services or work together to address an unmet need
    B. To gather and distribute information to consumers and agencies about unmet needs
    C. To publicize existing community resources and make them more accessible
    D. To bring an unmet community need to public attention in order to achieve acceptance of and support for fulfilling the need

26. Because of their clients' cultural background, social workers will most likely need to make some adjustments in learned attending skills when working with ____ clients.   26._____

    A. African American   B. Native American
    C. Southeast Asian-American   D. Pacific Islander

27. A social worker sees a client for several months for individual therapy, and then begins to see him in a group setting. The client expresses an interest in seeing his record. The social worker should   27._____

    A. provide the client with records, but warn him of his obligation to keep information about other group clients confidential
    B. deny the client access to the records due to the fact that they include information about other members of the group
    C. provide the client with those portions of the record that deal with him alone and don't mention other group members
    D. refer the client to the other group members, who must decide by consensus whether the client may view the record

28. Which of the following is NOT an assumption on which the solution-focused model of social work is built?   28._____

    A. It is not necessary to know the cause of a problem in order to solve it.
    B. Rapid change and rapid resolution of problems are possible.
    C. Clients usually resist changes, even though changes are rational and may provide relief.
    D. Only small positive changes are needed, due to the "ripple effect."

29. The core of any intervention contract is the   29._____

    A. specification of objectives   B. format
    C. identifying information   D. date of agreement

30. Which of the following is NOT a guideline that should be used by a social worker in summarizing during an interview?   30._____

    A. Summarize when a transition to new content is desirable.
    B. The content of summaries should be ordered in the same way that the client ordered it, in order to avoid confusion
    C. Wait to summarize until the content is sufficient to suggest a general theme.
    D. The client should participate in summarizing, either by summarizing him/herself, or by responding to the worker's summary.

31. During a crisis intervention, it is generally considered important to FIRST   31._____

    A. help the client to gain an intellectual understanding of the crisis
    B. help the client to establish or re-establish a social support system
    C. explore coping mechanisms
    D. help the client bring into the open his or her private feelings

32. "Attending" behaviors during interpersonal communication include each of the following, EXCEPT

    A. body squarely facing client
    B. body leaning slightly forward
    C. comfortable but not constant eye contact
    D. crossing arms or legs

33. A father of two contacts a social worker to seek foster care placement for his children. The reason, he explains, is that the children are placing a strain on his marriage, which is now experiencing serious problems, and he would like to have the time and space to address these problems with his wife. In an initial interview with this man, the worker should FIRST

    A. give the father the names and addresses of available foster care agencies
    B. conduct a problem search
    C. formulate a social support grid
    D. explain to him that his solution doesn't really fit the problem

34. A worker in the welfare department of a social services agency visits the home of a client who is a Food Stamp recipient, and asks if the client knows anyone who might need the services of a new agency program that provides meals and transportation for elderly citizens. The worker is reaching out through

    A. interviews and questionnaires
    B. field study needs assessment
    C. observation
    D. informal discussion with a community resident

35. When behavior modeling is used as a means of treatment, it is important to consider the factors that determine the likelihood that a model's behavior will be copied. Which of the following is NOT one of these?

    A. The observer's motivation to perform the modeled behavior
    B. The observer's retention of the modeled behavior
    C. The observer's ability to perform the behavior
    D. The willingness the observer's close relations to model the behavior

36. During an interview, a practitioner sometimes utters minimal encouragements ("uh-huh," "I see," "hmm") while a client is speaking. Usually, the effect of these essentially meaningless sounds is to

    A. distract the client from what he is trying to say
    B. assure the client that the practitioner is present and involved
    C. give the client the impression that the practitioner is only pretending to listen
    D. steer the client toward a particular topic or area of interest

37. A social worker can often enhance a client's problem-solving capacity by providing supportive and encouraging statements. Which of the following statements will typically be MOST helpful to a client?

    A. You are one of the most capable people I've ever met.
    B. After talking with your daughter, I think you're capable of taking on more parenting responsibilities.
    C. I'm sure you can do anything if you are determined enough.
    D. Based your recent job performance, I think you're due for a promotion.

38. A 19-year old man has just moved into a community. He dropped out of school at age 15, and has never had a job. He has found a place to live, but hasn't found work yet. When the man comes to the welfare agency and meets with a worker, he reacts angrily to the suggestion that he visit another worker about the possibility of enrolling in a youth employment program. Which of the following approaches by the worker would likely be LEAST helpful to the client at this point?

    A. Describing the types of resources available to assist him in locating a job
    B. Asking him about the reasons for his unwillingness to look for work
    C. Involving him in planning how to find and use a resource for locating a job
    D. Rehearsing with him ways of approaching a resource for help

39. During an initial interview, which of the following is typically NOT involved in the contracting process?

    A. Establishing the purpose of the contact
    B. Dealing with issues of authority
    C. Taking a social history
    D. Explaining the worker's role

40. Giving advice to clients is most helpful when it

    A. focuses on means, rather than ends
    B. is general, rather than specific in nature
    C. is offered in a way that the client doesn't realize she is being given advice
    D. follows the worker's explanation of why previous solutions have failed

41. During their meetings together a battered wife and a social worker have agreed to focus on the decision of whether the wife should return to her husband or end her marriage. The worker should help the client to

    A. convince the husband to attend joint sessions in order to reach a conclusion
    B. engage in role reversal
    C. recognize the difference between means and ends
    D. construct a decision-making matrix weighing the costs and benefits of each option

42. Which of the following is an informal resource system?

    A. A Salvation Army Center
    B. A privately owned day care center
    C. Neighbors of parents of developmentally disabled clients
    D. A Boy Scout troop interested in volunteering to help the developmentally disabled

43. A practitioner is using the listening technique of paraphrasing to help a young mother develop an understanding of her situation. When the client says, "I should never have become a mother," the MOST helpful paraphrasing reply that could be used by the practitioner is

   A. You shouldn't have become a parent.
   B. Your children are a burden to you.
   C. Why do you say you should never have become a mother?
   D. You don't like being a mother.

44. Most agencies and programs prohibit the use of punishment as a means of determining behavior. Which of the following is NOT a reason for this?

   A. The results of punishment are usually short-term.
   B. It appears to have little or no effect on an individual's behavior.
   C. It provides a poor behavioral model for the client.
   D. Desirable behaviors may also be suppressed by punishment.

45. An eighty-year-old man and his family have recently learned that he has inoperable brain cancer, and his prognosis is poor. His wife and son are reacting very differently; the son wants to keep his father alive by any means necessary, and the mother is in complete denial about the situation. Neither the son nor the wife have the resources necessary for a long course of treatment, and the patient is covered only by Medicaid. The patient is aware of this, and worries that he might be a burden to his family. He has read recent articles about assisted suicide, and wants to discuss it with the medical social worker at the hospital. The social worker should FIRST

   A. make the family aware of advance directives such is living wills and health care proxies
   B. alert local law enforcement officials that the client is considering an illegal procedure
   C. seek resources and social supports that would help the family deal with the emotional and financial consequences of a prolonged death
   D. inform the family of all the possible medical courses of action, and then encourage them to make their own decisions

46. In general, the BEST preventive support to families at risk for child abuse or neglect is provided by

   A. community natural helpers
   B. self-help groups
   C. individual caseworkers
   D. formal interagency programs

47. In client interviews, supportive statements by the practitioner are MOST likely to be effective if he or she can

   A. set aside feelings of disapproval for other client behaviors
   B. identify the client's feeling or the behavior for which the practitioner is expressing approval or encouragement
   C. use the statement to steer the client toward a specific course of action
   D. differentiate between the times when a client is genuinely hurting and when he/she is simply trying to gain sympathy

48. A practitioner visits a hospital for an interview with a young woman who is struggling with anorexia nervosa. This young woman's problem could most usefully be framed as

    A. a problem in decision-making
    B. a psychological and behavioral problem
    C. dissatisfaction in social relations
    D. a problem of social transition

49. An example of a "remedial" group is one that is

    A. focused on helping couples learn to communicate better
    B. focused on teaching parents child nurturing skills
    C. developed for adolescents who have been involved in delinquent behavior
    D. an inpatient group for chemically dependent patients

50. A supervisor of medical social services staff assigns a worker to cases in the Geriatric Ward. The large number of delusional and feeble older people in the ward has been disturbing to the worker, who some years ago lost her father after a long bout with Alzheimer's disease. After being assigned a case involving an older man with Alzheimer's disease, the worker meets with the supervisor, explains her problem, and requests reassignment to another case. In evaluating the worker's request, the supervisor should weigh the worker's strong negative feelings about the case against the

    A. unhealthy precedent set by allowing workers to reject specific case assignments
    B. client's need for immediate intervention
    C. worker's capacity for growth through experience
    D. worker's proven ability to deal with a variety of geriatric cases

51. In general, outpatient drug- or alcohol-dependency treatment programs are considered appropriate for young people
    I. who have family members who are willing to participate
    II. who are willing to abstain from illicit drug use and submit to urine testing with accompanying psychiatric problems
    III. with unrelated chronic medical problems

    A. I only
    B. I and II
    C. I and II
    D. I II, III and IV

52. The "middle" phase of a professional social worker/client relationship is typically characterized by each of the following, EXCEPT

    A. acceptance and honesty
    B. constant movement and change
    C. uncertainty and exploration
    D. goal-orientation

53. An Asian American client meets with a social worker and says he is thinking of dropping out of school to work on troubles he is having with his girlfriend. The social worker has known the client for several months, is acquainted with his goals and ambitions, and thinks this is a bad idea. The BEST approach with a client from an Asian cultural background in this case would probably be to respond by saying:

   A. Are you saying that this girlfriend is more important than school?
   B. How do you think that might affect your future?
   C. I wonder if your response is appropriate given the situation here.
   D. Dropping out now will affect your financial aid and your ability to take classes next semester.

54. An agency attempts to evaluate community satisfaction with social services. It realizes that 88% of the people in the community are African-American, while the others in the community are of other ethnic groups. In making sure that exactly 88% of the replies to its surveys are from African-Americans, the agency is practicing

   A. random sampling
   B. targeted sampling
   C. the focus-group technique
   D. stratified random sampling

55. Which of the following is generally TRUE?

   A. The onset of alcoholism among parents is most likely to occur after the birth of a second child.
   B. Male relatives of alcoholics are at greater risk of alcoholism than female relatives.
   C. It is rare to have only one alcoholic member in a family; there are usually two or more.
   D. The member who suffers from alcoholism is usually a parent.

56. When interviewing a client, a social worker may sometimes make use of the questioning technique known as the "reaction probe." The purpose of this technique is to

   A. point out inadequately covered content
   B. increase the emotional depth of the interview
   C. provoke an affective reaction from the client
   D. elicit a clearer explanation of personal situations

57. An elderly married couple visits a practitioner to discuss the rising costs of their prescription drugs. During their meeting the husband says: "The costs are killing us. We had no choice but to come here because Medicare just won't cover all the prescriptions we need." A practitioner who is using the listening technique of reflecting feeling would

   A. pound the table and say, "That makes me angry!"
   B. say nothing, but look steadily at the wife until she answers
   C. say: "You need to apply for supplementary coverage because your prescription costs are rising."
   D. say: "You seem to feel uncomfortable and unhappy about having to seek help."

58. The primary disadvantage associated with use of the word "diagnosis" in social work assessment is that

    A. workers tend to focus on what is wrong with the family, client, or group
    B. it is often harmful to the client's self-esteem
    C. it lends an air of medical authority to the worker's recorded observations
    D. a collateral problem system may be ignored entirely

59. Which of the following is an example of indirect macro practice?

    A. Lobbying a state legislature for more funding for public housing
    B. Researching the causes and impacts of community housing problems
    C. Working to find housing for a recently evicted client
    D. Advocating on behalf of a community for better housing

60. Which of the following is a provision of the NASW code of ethics regarding social work with groups and families?

    A. Social workers should inform clients that there is no guarantee that all participants will honor confidentiality.
    B. Social workers should limit themselves to an explanation of the agency's policy regarding confidentiality.
    C. Social workers should assure clients that confidentiality will be protected.
    D. If confidentiality is breached, social workers will share with the group or family members what has been discussed by individual members

61. A child is able to identify his father, even though his father's back is turned. According to Piaget, this child has achieved

    A. object permanence
    B. synthesis
    C. object constancy
    D. assimilation

62. When a professional social worker/client relationship is described as "dynamic," this means that it

    A. may have become too volatile for the worker or client to handle
    B. is constantly changing
    C. demands that both or all of the people involved participate actively in the process
    D. is always the source of positive feelings and thoughts

63. A social worker says to a young client "You say your teacher hates you and wants you to fail. But you just told me she offered to stay after school to go over the assignment with you, and recommended a tutor. How does that add up? I don't get it." The social worker is using the technique of

    A. summarization
    B. paraphrasing
    C. confrontation
    D. interpretation

64. A Vietnamese family visits a social worker for the first time. The father's name is Cao Dinh Phong. The social worker should address this man as

    A. Mr. Phong
    B. Mr. Cao
    C. Dinh Phong
    D. Cao

65. The use of the DSM-V in client assessment is likely to involve each of the following benefits, EXCEPT

    A. a means for professionals to communicate with each other about specific client problems
    B. its usefulness in teaching about mental disorders
    C. a means for identifying causes of specific client problems
    D. helpfulness in evaluating and treating clients with mental disorders

66. A social worker may comply with a request by a supervisor automatically, without any thought of the supervisor's motives for the request. In assuming that the supervisor's request was legitimate, the worker is responding to power.

    A. coercive
    B. expert
    C. positional
    D. referent

67. Each of the following statements about Spanish-speaking families is generally true, EXCEPT

    A. The boundaries of nuclear families are flexible.
    B. Most do not experience an "empty nest" stage.
    C. There is a high percentage of single-parent families.
    D. There is no stigma attached to a parent who relinquishes a child for the sake of its future.

68. According to the NASW code of ethics, social workers who believe a colleague's probably alcoholism is impairing his or her practice should

    A. first report concerns to the state licensing board
    B. report concerns to the appropriate supervisor
    C. advise the colleague to seek professional help
    D. consult with the colleague and take additional steps if necessary

69. A social worker begins an assessment of a client by listing the client's own characteristics in the following way: "Education (-); Religion (+); Self-Reliance (-).. ." The worker is making use of

    A. the dual perspective
    B. projection
    C. ecomapping
    D. emotion-focused coping strategies

70. During an early group work session, one member in particular seems intent on expressing her independence from the group members, and in making overt attempts to assume a leadership role. This member would be described as

    A. counterdependent
    B. authoritarian
    C. codependent
    D. unpaired

71. Advantages of the use of open-ended questions in client interviews include
    I. maximizing client freedom regarding content
    II. providing client's cognitive and affective views of problem
    III. easier format for inexperienced interviewers
    IV. maximizing worker access to desirable data

    A. I and II
    B. I, II and III
    C. III only
    D. I, II, III and IV

72. Which of the factors is NOT believed to have contributed to the "feminization" of poverty over the past 15-20 years?

    A. The labor market created by new information technologies
    B. A welfare system that functions to perpetuate dependency
    C. Weakening of the nuclear family
    D. Rapid growth of female-headed families

73. "Boundary-spanning" skills in social work administration are involved in the role(s) of
    I. broker
    II. innovator
    III. researcher
    IV. enabler

    A. I and II
    B. II and IV
    C. III only
    D. I, II, III and IV

74. During the assessment process, a social worker can maintain a focus on client strengths in each of the following ways, EXCEPT

    A. formulating an intervention plan that is specific and individualized
    B. receiving client statements with a degree of skepticism that is scaled to the intensity of emotion that accompanies it
    C. helping the client identify and articulate his/her expectations of the worker and agency
    D. assuming that the client is an expert on his or her behavior

75. In which of the following situations is the use of "small talk" in an opening interview MOST likely to be contraindicated?

    A. Referral for ongoing marital problems
    B. Home visit to a general assistance client
    C. Family crisis intervention
    D. Court-ordered anger management counseling

KEY (CORRECT ANSWERS)

1.	C	16.	C	31.	A	46.	A	61.	C
2.	A	17.	D	32.	D	47.	B	62.	C
3.	D	18.	C	33.	B	48.	B	63.	C
4.	A	19.	B	34.	D	49.	D	64.	A
5.	A	20.	A	35.	D	50.	C	65.	C
6.	A	21.	B	36.	B	51.	B	66.	C
7.	D	22.	D	37.	B	52.	C	67.	C
8.	A	23.	C	38.	B	53.	D	68.	D
9.	C	24.	D	39.	C	54.	D	69.	A
10.	C	25.	B	40.	A	55.	B	70.	A
11.	B	26.	B	41.	D	56.	B	71.	A
12.	B	27.	C	42.	C	57.	D	72.	A
13.	D	28.	C	43.	D	58.	A	73.	A
14.	B	29.	A	44.	B	59.	B	74.	B
15.	D	30.	B	45.	C	60.	A	75.	C

TEST 2

DIRECTIONS: Each question or incomplete statement is followed by several suggested answers or completions. Select the one that BEST answers the question or completes the statement. *PRINT THE LETTER OF THE CORRECT ANSWER IN THE SPACE AT THE RIGHT.*

1. Under the most recent NASW code of ethics, confidentiality requirements
   A. prevent the use of case materials for educational purposes
   B. apply only to oral or written case reports
   C. are extended to include computers and fax machines
   D. no longer apply to clients who are deceased

2. The first stage of any two-parent family life cycle is most often characterized by
   A. boundary negotiation
   B. subsystem formation
   C. power sharing
   D. triangulation

3. Of all the techniques at a practitioner's disposal, the ones most likely to be misused are
   A. advice giving and counseling
   B. confrontation
   C. universalization
   D. differential diagnosis

4. A social worker is assigned the task of planning an intervention for a client with a serious mental illness. Which of the following models of social work practice is MOST appropriate for this client?
   A. Psychodynamic
   B. Person-centered
   C. Clubhouse
   D. Cognitive-behavioral

5. A mother who appears to live, through her children, and who suppresses her own needs in light of theirs, is described as
   A. deviant
   B. Marianist
   C. ordinal
   D. allocentric

6. During an assessment interview, a client describes his relationship with his mother as shaky and uncertain. In putting together an ecomap of this client and his environment, the social worker would depict this relationship by using a(n)
   A. line with several vertical hashmarks (-I-I-I-I-I-)
   B. arrow pointing away from the mother, toward the client
   C. dotted line
   D. heavy black line

7. For a social services agency, advantages of cost-reimbursable contracts include

   I. Possibility of surpluses if programs are well-managed
   II. Greater autonomy from contracting agency
   III. Guaranteed quality-of-service levels
   IV. Limited financial exposure of social service agency

   A. I and II
   B. II and III
   C. IV only
   D. I, II, III and IV

8. In general, child and teen delinquency rates are highest among

   A. the poor and the working class
   B. the working class and the middle class
   C. the middle class
   D. the poor and the very rich

9. In most human service teams, the leadership role frequently involves each of the following functions, EXCEPT that of

   A. administrator/evaluator
   B. logistics
   C. team/client broker
   D. liaison with host institution

10. A single mother and her teenage son visit a social worker to seek resolution for what they see as nearly constant conflict. The son begins the interview by saying of the mother: "She hates me. All she does is yell at me. I don't even want to be around her any more." The BEST way for the practitioner to respond to this statement would be:

    A. Sometimes there might be good reasons for your mother to be upset. What do you think those might be?
    B. You sound upset about how much she yells at you. Do you think she might be hurt and upset also?
    C. What do you do just before your mother yells at you?
    D. Do you think your mother hates you and doesn't want to be around you, either?

11. Generally, a professional social worker/client relationship is LEAST likely to be

    A. formal and structured
    B. limited in time
    C. emotional
    D. unequal

12. Many clients prefer the use of informal helping resources over formal ones. Which of the following is a reason for this?

    A. Easy professional access
    B. No stigma attached
    C. Improved client confidentiality
    D. Greater specificity in matched services

13. NASW code of ethics provisions regarding the roles of supervisors and administrators include
    I. an advisement against any reduction in the number of agency caseworkers
    II. limits on the number of workers that can be supervised by an individual
    III. responsibility of administrators and supervisors for providing continuing education for their staff
    IV. the annual conduct of staff evaluations

    A. I and II
    B. II, III and IV
    C. III only
    D. I, II, III and IV

    13.____

14. Which of the following words would NOT typically be used to describe spoken communication?

    A. Dynamic
    B. Transactional
    C. Contextual
    D. Reversible

    14.____

15. A teenager with school achievement problems spends much time on the telephone with her friends after school. Together, the social worker and the girl's parents decide to reward her for every hour she spends studying during after-school hours, and to ignore whatever time she spends on the telephone. This is an example of a(n) _____ reinforcement schedule.

    A. intermittent
    B. random
    C. differential
    D. continuous

    15.____

16. The termination of a professional social worker/client relationship should accomplish three things. Which of the following is NOT typically one of these things?

    A. Setting ground rules for future contacts
    B. Providing direction for the future
    C. Dealing with feelings about termination
    D. Dealing with unfinished business

    16.____

17. During a group session involving several members of alcoholic families, a practitioner attempts to steer members toward the issue of family violence with a question about how one member, a teenage daughter, felt while her father was in jail after an episode. The daughter begins to talk about the incident in a very general way, and within a few minutes she and another teenage daughter are involved in a conversation about mutual acquaintances at school. Nobody in the group seems to be making any attempt to interrupt them; in fact, they seem to be enjoying the conversation. According to Bion, this group could be described as a(n) _____ group.

    A. pairing
    B. night-fight
    C. conflicted
    D. counterdependent

    17.____

18. Which of the following is NOT a general guideline to be followed by social workers who are engaged in advocacy?

    A. If possible, help the client him/herself argue the case rather than speaking on behalf.
    B. Write down all intended questions and statements prior to contacting agency representatives.
    C. Realize that advocacy can damage established interagency relationships, and weigh the risks against other possible solutions.
    D. When contacting another agency, attempt to speak to the person at the highest administrative level possible.

19. A practitioner begins the treatment process for an alcoholic family that has just experienced a crisis. In the beginning stages of work, after contracting with family members to work together to improve their communication skills, the practitioner should

    A. focus the intervention on the alcoholic and identify other family members' roles in relation to that person
    B. test hunches about family interactions with the family members, to see whether they challenge them or agree to some extent
    C. observe the family to identify their idiosyncratic language
    D. work with the family to determine who the "identified patient" is

20. During a therapeutic interview, a client expresses deep regrets over past behaviors that resulted from her drinking problem. She speaks on this subject for several minutes, and then stops and looks at the practitioner. In order to demonstrate good attending behavior, the BEST response on the part of the practitioner would be to

    A. reply immediately with a question
    B. reply immediately with a statement of support
    C. wait indefinitely, maintaining eye contact, for the client to continue
    D. wait two to five seconds, and then give a reply

21. A practitioner works to make clients feel as if their relationship with a treatment group is one of interdependence and mutual strength. In group social work, this is known as the

    A. outreach program
    B. medical model
    C. psychology of oppression
    D. symbiotic assumption

22. Which of the following is a formal resource system?

    A. Relatives of nursing home residents
    B. A Girl Scout troop interested in volunteering to help nursing home residents
    C. Special classes offered for the elderly offered through the local public schools
    D. A privately owned nursing home

23. Given current knowledge about genetics, the tendency toward alcoholism or other chemical addictions is best described as a(n)

    A. polygenic disorder, due to the additive effects of a number of genes
    B. structural chromosomal defect
    C. single-gene, autosomal dominant disorder
    D. X-linked disorder

24. During an assessment interview, a father who has been convicted of physically abusing his son states that the reason for the abuse was because "that's all he understands." In this case, the father is practicing

    A. rationalization
    B. intellectualizauon
    C. a task-focused coping strategy
    D. an emotion-focused coping strategy

25. A client with chronic undifferentiated schizophrenia, now in a halfway house with other discharged psychiatric patients, tells a social worker of her desire to seek custody of her child. The child was born to her a year earlier in a psychiatric hospital and is now in foster care, awaiting adoption. The client currently exhibits no acute psychotic symptoms and is taking all prescribed medications. The social worker should

    A. advocate for the client to the foster care and adoption agencies
    B. ask the foster care agency to arrange for supervised visits between the client and her child, so that her ability to care for the child can be evaluated
    C. ask the foster care agency to arrange for unsupervised visits between the client and her child, in order to respect the client's right to self-determination
    D. advise the client that because of the nature of her illness, her child will probably never be returned to her

26. A child who is physically abused generally does NOT

    A. exhibit serious behavioral problems
    B. exhibit hyper-vigilant or guarded behavior
    C. have bruises that are in different stages of healing
    D. show off injuries or bruises to other children

27. In general, guidelines for cross-cultural interviews in social work include
    I.   the use of summarizing in interviews
    II. focusing on closed rather than open questions
    III. remembering that not all cultures value openness and authenticity
    IV. extensive use of self-disclosure to increase client comfort

    A. I only   B. I and II
    C. II, III and IV   D. I, II, III and IV

28. The most significant difference between a data-gathering tool and an assessment tool is that

   A. an assessment tool makes use of direct questioning
   B. an assessment tool incorporates a scaling procedure
   C. a data-gathering tool requires special training for implementation
   D. a data-gathering tool is standardized

29. An instrument designed to test for depression is given to a group of patients already hospitalized for depression. If their scores in the instrument are low, indicating a depressed state, the instrument has demonstrated

   A. reliability
   B. predictive validity
   C. face validity
   D. concurrent validity

30. The highest proportion of problem drinkers among women are generally to be found in the _____ -year-old age group.

   A. 10 to 15
   B. 16 to 20
   C. 21 to 34
   D. 35 to 49

31. A 65-year-old man has been in a state penitentiary for the last 20 years, and is now being prepared for release. In an initial interview, the worker discovers that the man has no relatives, no means of financial support, and no place to live. The man has made it clear that he wants to live by himself and find some way of meeting older people in his community. The FIRST thing the worker should do is

   A. escort the man to an appointment with a housing service
   B. explore the man's unwillingness to enter a boarding home
   C. discuss the man's situation directly, explaining the resources that might be useful for assistance
   D. contact several available resources and inquire about their ability to help

32. Common adult behavior patterns that indicate the possibility of past child abuse include

   I. submissiveness
   II. being out of touch with one's own needs
   III. low self-esteem
   IV. excessive efforts to please others

   A. I and IV
   B. II and III
   C. I, III and IV
   D. I, II, III and IV

33. Which of the following activities is involved in the social worker's task of mobilizing?

   A. Meeting individuals in the community with problems and assisting them in finding help
   B. Identifying unmet community needs
   C. Speaking out against an unjust policy or procedure
   D. Developing new services or linking presently available services to meet community needs

34. Beliefs that are important to the feminist perspective of social work include each of the following, EXCEPT

    A. helping limited to advocacy
    B. sharing of social worker's relevant experiences
    C. egalitarian client-social worker relationship
    D. assessment of client problems within a sociopolitical context

35. Which of the following results are likely among families with an adolescent child in which the parents have not worked out their own issues regarding separation?
    I. The adolescent becomes staunchly self-sufficient and seeks employment or schooling early as a means of leaving.
    II. Parents may infantilize the adolescent, keeping him or her overly dependent and close.
    III. Parents may detach their child from the family prematurely, forcing him or her from the home.

    A. I and II
    B. I and III
    C. II and III
    D. I, II, and III

36. A social worker is asked by an attorney to reveal information about a client. Assuming there are no laws to the contrary, a social worker should NEVER feel obligated to reveal information about

    A. a client's immigration status
    B. what is discussed during treatment sessions
    C. the projected duration of a client's treatment
    D. behavior that led to a client's involuntary hospitalization

37. A group begins with an idea, amends it repeatedly to satisfy divergent points of view, and then approves the final product. The group has reached a decision through

    A. consensus
    B. majority
    C. compromise
    D. persuasion

38. Each of the following is a guideline for offering advice during client interviews, EXCEPT

    A. Advice should be given in conjunction with other interventions whenever possible.
    B. Advice should be offered only after helping clients explore their own suggestions.
    C. The request for advice must come clearly from the client, and not an outgrowth of the worker's needs.
    D. If advice is offered, it should be offered firmly, with little chance for rejection.

39. A supervisor receives a call from an angry client who is upset about a caseworker's decision to deny visitation to her (the client's) child, who has been placed in foster care. After looking into the matter, the supervisor agrees with the worker's decision. The supervisor should

    A. ignore the matter and let the worker handle it
    B. call the client, tell her of his support for the decision, and arrange a meeting between the three of them to talk it over
    C. call and inform the worker that the client is upset
    D. call the foster family and warn them of the client's anger

39.____

40. Which of the following groups are generally MOST vulnerable to the onset of alcohol- or drug-dependencies?

    A. School-age children and adolescents
    B. Adolescents and young adult men
    C. Adolescents and middle-aged women
    D. Young adult men and women

40.____

41. The legal definition of "privileged communication" between a worker and a client relies on several criteria, including

    I. The communication must originate in the belief that it will not be disclosed
    II. The inviolability of the confidence must be essential to achieve the purpose of the relationship
    III. The relationship must be one that society would foster
    IV. The expected injury to the relationship through disclosure must be greater than the expected benefit to justice if the witness were forced to testify

    A. I and II
    B. I, II and III
    C. II, III, and IV
    D. I, II, III and IV

41.____

42. The term "social action" is used to denote each of the following, EXCEPT

    A. working in local and national elections to elect sympathetic representatives
    B. networking with other groups pursuing a similar agenda
    C. pursuing a legislative agenda designed to meet large-scale problems with large-scale programs
    D. advocacy around specific populations and issues such as the homeless and hunger

42.____

43. In the "ABC" model of behavioral intervention, the "A" stands for

    A addressing
    B. antecedent
    C. appropriate
    D. access

43.____

44. Which stage of the development of a public policy issue involves the enactment of laws and regulations?

    A. Visibility
    B. Clarification
    C. Development
    D. Action

44.____

45. The basic formula for writing intervention objectives includes each of the following items, EXCEPT

    A. how
    B. when
    C. who
    D. what

46. The concept of "permanency planning" refers to social services in

    A. clients with developmental disabilities
    B. child welfare
    C. dual relationships
    D. substance abuse

47. Which of the following is NOT generally a guideline that should be followed in the assessment process?

    A. Assessment must be an ongoing process.
    B. Assessment always involves making subjective judgments.
    C. Client involvement in assessment is absolutely essential.
    D. The problem should always be reduced to a single, clear definition.

48. In client interviews, the listening technique of paraphrasing is generally useful for each of the following purposes, EXCEPT

    A. forcing the practitioner to focus on the most important aspects of statements
    B. helping clients to finish expressing uncompleted or unclear thoughts
    C. highlighting significant aspects of client statements
    D. helping clients to see more clearly what they have said

49. Social work supervisors assume a consistent difference between professional and non-professional activities. In general, professional activities are

    A. predictable
    B. standardized
    C. specific
    D. idiosyncratic

50. Which of the following is NOT an assumption involved in the structural-functional approach to family treatment?

    A. The family as social system serves both the individual and the society.
    B. Each stage of family development involves a discrete set of tasks to be mastered.
    C. A family is a social system with functional requirements.
    D. A family is a small group with generic features common to all small groups.

51. Closed questions are appropriate during a client interview when

    I. some details are missing from client statements
    II. the situation appears confusing
    III. the worker needs to generate some momentum for the interview
    IV. the client is uncertain about how to proceed

    A. I only
    B. I, III and IV
    C. II and IV
    D. I, II, III and IV

52. Used as a response during a client interview, reflection of feeling can have the effect of
    I. giving sanction to negative emotions
    II. assuring the client that the worker is trying to understand
    III. reinforcing the discussion of feelings
    IV. clarifying unclear sensations

    A. I, II and IV
    B. II and III
    C. IV only
    D. I, II, III and IV

53. A practitioner meets with the family of a recently-paralyzed teenager to decide whether to place him in his own home, a group home, or some other residential setting. This family's problem could most usefully be framed as

    A. a problem of decision-making
    B. inadequate resources
    C. interpersonal conflict
    D. a problem of social transition

54. Which of the following is a form of front-end analysis?

    A. Client satisfaction questionnaire
    B. Process analysis
    C. Needs assessment
    D. Single-subject (AB) design

55. Which of the following is a basic presumption of behaviorist theory?

    A. People are pleasure-seeking creatures.
    B. The organization of behavior becomes qualitatively different from one period of a person's life span to the next
    C. Security is a major goal in a person's life.
    D. People are basically emotional and irrational.

56. Which of the following is a good reason for a practitioner to make use of a transition during an interview?

    A. The worker does not feel comfortable either agreeing or disagreeing with a provocative client statement, and prefers to move on.
    B. The worker is aware that the agency will be unable to meet the needs being expressed by the client.
    C. The client is sharing material of a more emotional nature than is desirable at this point in the contract.
    D. The client does not provide an answer that is either expected or useful.

57. In general, clients from an Asian cultural background will respond well to an intervention approach that is

    A. collaborative
    B. directive
    C. experiential
    D. client-centered

58. A social worker asks a woman who has been receiving AFDC benefits how her disabled husband feels about her going back to work. The woman says he's completely behind her. The worker replies: "Completely behind you?" In this instance, the worker is using reflection as a specific questioning technique known as the

    A. reaction probe
    B. completion probe
    C. leading question
    D. clarity probe

59. Which of the following terms is used to denote the decision clients make to deal with their most difficult issues as they approach the end of a working relationship with a practitioner?

    A. Stage identity
    B. Key decision
    C. End resolve
    D. Third decision

60. A child gives a one-word command to an adult: "Juice," indicating that the child wants a drink and needs the adult's assistance. The function of the child's language in this case is

    A. personal
    B. regulatory
    C. instrumental
    D. interactional

61. A family intervention modeled on the Child At Risk Held System (CARF) typically involves

    A. the abuser alone
    B. the abuser and the child or children who suffer the abuse
    C. both parents, assuming one is the abuser, and the abused child(ren)
    D. the entire family

62. In group social work, one member may tend to intervene each time the discussion nears a painful subject This group member is known as the

    A. gatekeeper
    B. internal leader
    C. scapegoat
    D. deviant member

63. Typically, the FIRST step in a community needs assessment is

    A. identifying community's strengths
    B. exploring the nature of the neighborhood
    C. getting to know the area and its residents
    D. talking to people in the community

64. During an interview, a teenage boy says: "I know I haven't been easy to live with my schoolwork's been bad, and I've been running around a lot. Maybe doing some drugs. My parents were unhappy and they gave me a hard time about it. But I don't see why they had to get a divorce." The practitioner responds: "You're pretty honest about how you contributed to those family problems. But why do you blame yourself for your parents' divorce?" In this case, the practitioner is making an attempt at

    A. reflection   B. interpretation   C. summarizing   D. confrontation

65. A social worker, fearing countertransference, wants to videotape his group bereavement sessions in order to review his interactions with a supervisor. When asked for consent, all but one of the group members agrees. The social worker should

   A. assume a majority and tape the sessions
   B. not tape the sessions under any circumstances, even if the dissenting group member is not present
   C. tape only those group sessions that are not attended by the dissenting group member
   D. refer the dissenting client to another group

66. According to Alfred Adler, the prime motivator for people to strive to improve skills and behaviors is

   A. feelings of inferiority
   B. desire for pleasure
   C. need for security
   D. desire for love

67. Which of the following offers the BEST description of the target of a crisis intervention?

   A. Displays of emotion
   B. Attitudes about loss
   C. Long-term consequences
   D. Specific, observable difficulties

68. As part of a proposal for funding, a social work agency's organizational overview typically contains each of the following, EXCEPT

   A. current audited financial statements
   B. the agency mission statement
   C. description of constituency
   D. current activities

69. In generalist practice, workers should be wary of several factors when using the DSM-IV as an assessment tool. Which of the following is NOT one of these factors?

   A. There is a tendency to focus on individual pathology.
   B. It doesn't provide any recommendations for treatment or intervention strategies.
   C. There is a tendency toward oversimplification when a client has several complex problems.
   D. Generalizations about environmental factors are often inaccurate or irrelevant to specific cases.

70. The most effective approach for dealing with alcoholic clients is usually

   A. confrontation
   B. negative reinforcement
   C. punishment
   D. family sculpting

71. A worker who wants a more open-ended answer from a client would be most successful by using questions that begin with

   A. what or how
   B. is or was
   C. when or why
   D. have or had

72. Which of the following statements about early and prolonged malnutrition is generally TRUE?

    A. When accompanied by minimal stimulation, it impairs brain growth and intellectual development.
    B. The effects of prolonged malnutrition are irreversible past the age of about ten.
    C. Regardless of mental stimulation, it will lead to impaired mental development
    D. Its effects are more observable as emotional than intellectual.

72.____

73. Under the NASW code's provision on cultural competency, social workers are urged to
    I. develop an understanding of clients' cultural backgrounds
    II. make arrangements to have interpreters available for non-English-speaking clients
    III. be mindful of how diagnosis may be affected by ethnic background
    IV. have an ethnic background similar to that of case clients

    A. I only
    B. I and II
    C. I, II and III
    D. I, II, III and IV

73.____

74. When working with a Latino family, a social worker having little experience or knowledge of Latino culture is at risk for making the assumption that

    A. fathers are overinvolved in the lives of their children
    B. children have little regard for their parents
    C. family boundaries are too rigidly defined
    D. families in general are passive and nonaggressive in dealing with issues

74.____

75. Which of the following should typically NOT be an objective of a worker's self-disclosure during a client interview?

    A. Facilitating the client's willingness to communicate
    B. Modeling appropriate behavior for the client
    C. Pointing out an appropriate resolution or course of action
    D. Provoking a catharsis for the client

75.____

KEY (CORRECT ANSWERS)

1. C	16. A	31. C	46. B	61. D
2. A	17. A	32. D	47. D	62. A
3. A	18. D	33. D	48. B	63. B
4. C	19. C	34. A	49. D	64. B
5. D	20. D	35. C	50. B	65. B
6. C	21. D	36. A	51. D	66. A
7. C	22. B	37. C	52. D	67. D
8. D	23. A	38. D	53. A	68. A
9. C	24. A	39. B	54. C	69. D
10. B	25. B	40. C	55. A	70. A
11. A	26. D	41. D	56. C	71. A
12. B	27. A	42. C	57. B	72. A
13. C	28. B	43. B	58. D	73. A
14. D	29. D	44. D	59. D	74. D
15. A	30. D	45. A	60. C	75. C

EXAMINATION SECTION
TEST 1

DIRECTIONS: Each question or incomplete statement is followed by several suggested answers or completions. Select the one that BEST answers the question or completes the statement. *PRINT THE LETTER OF THE CORRECT ANSWER IN THE SPACE AT THE RIGHT.*

1. Assume that you are a supervisor recently assigned to a new unit. You notice that, for the past few days, one of the employees in your unit whose work is about average has been stopping work at about four o'clock and has been spending the rest of the afternoon relaxing at his desk.
   The BEST of the following actions for you to take in this situation is to
   A. assign more work to this employee since it is apparent that he does not have enough work to keep him busy
   B. observe the employee's conduct more closely for about ten days before taking any more positive action
   C. discuss the matter with the employee, pointing out to him how he can use the extra hour daily to raise the level of his job performance
   D. question the previous supervisor in charge of the unit in order to determine whether he had sanctioned such conduct when he supervised that unit

1.____

2. A supervisor, newly assigned in charge of a small project, discovers that the previous supervisor and one of the employees supervised by him put all their business communications with each other in written form. The newly assigned supervisor finds that the employee is continuing to put his communications in writing and has requested that the supervisor do the same in order to prevent misunderstandings.
   It would generally be BEST for the supervisor to
   A. accede to the request since the likelihood of misunderstandings will be reduced and since, as a newly assigned supervisor, he should not make changes until he is well established and accepted
   B. allow the employee to communicate with him in the way in which he chooses but refuse to communicate with the employee in writing except in cases where he would generally consider written communications to be desirable, on the grounds that too much of the supervisor's time would be wasted thereby
   C. inform the employee that neither one of them is to use written communications excessively in order to reduce the time consumed by communication but with the understanding that the employee may resort to writing in cases where he has serious reason to fear a misunderstanding
   D. instruct the employee to cease the use of written communications in excess of the use of them by the other employees and refuses to accede to his request since the result would be an excessive waste of time

2.____

3. A policy of direct crosswise communication on a project between a member of the management staff and a member of the maintenance staff of equal or superior status rather than following the chain of command upward through the manager and down through the top maintenance supervisor is a policy to be
   A. *discouraged*, primarily because it places responsibility where it does not belong and makes the quality of communication erratic and undependable
   B. *discouraged*, primarily because the manager and upper level supervisors will fail to receive the full information they need to make policy and administrative decisions
   C. *encouraged*, primarily because it results in decision making at the lowest practical level
   D. *encouraged*, primarily because it shortens the communication time and improves the quality of communication

4. A supervisor in a large department should be thoroughly familiar with modern methods of personnel administration. This statement is
   A. *true*, because this familiarity will help him in performing the normal functions of his office
   B. *false*, because in a large city personnel administration is not a departmental matter, but is centralized in a civil service commission
   C. *true*, because this knowledge will insure the elimination of personnel problems in a department
   D. *false*, because the departmental problems of a minor character are handled by the personnel representative, while major problems are the responsibility of the commissioner

5. The LEAST true of the following is that a supervisor in a large department
   A. executes the policy laid down by the commissioner or his deputies
   B. in the main, carries out the policies of the commissioner but with some leeway where his own frame of reference is determinative
   C. is never required to formulate policy
   D. is responsible for the successful accomplishment of a section of the department's program

6. In the supervision of young inexperienced investigators, the MOST important training task for the supervisor is to
   A. encourage investigators to make their own decisions about case problems
   B. give experience-based answers to various problems that arise in cases
   C. teach investigators how to analyze and assess important facts in order to make decisions about case problems
   D. teach investigators how to recognize evidence of mental breakdown

7. The supervisor is responsible for the accuracy of the work performed by his subordinates. Of the following procedures which he might adopt to insure the accurate copying of long reports from rough draft originals, the MOST effective one is to
   A. examine the rough draft for errors in grammar, punctuation, and spelling before assigning it to a typist to copy

B. glance through each typed report before it leaves his bureau to detect any obvious errors made by the typist
C. have another employee read the rough draft original to the typist who typed the report, and have the typist make whatever corrections are necessary
D. rotate assignments involving the typing of long reports equally among all the typists in the unit

8. In the course of your duties, you receive a letter which, you believe, should be called to the attention of your superior.
Of the following, the BEST reason for attaching previous correspondence to this letter before giving it to your superior is that
   A. there is less danger, if such a procedure is followed, of misplacing important letters
   B. this letter can probably be better understood in the light of previous correspondence
   C. your supervisor is probably in a better position to understand the letter than you
   D. this letter will have to be filed eventually so there is no additional work involved

8._____

9. The most successful supervisor wins his victories through preventive rather than through curative action.
The one of the following which is the MOST accurate statement on the basis of this counsel is that
   A. success in supervision may be measured more accurately in terms of errors corrected than in terms of errors prevented
   B. anticipating problems makes for better supervision than waiting until problems arise
   C. difficulties that cannot be prevented by the supervisor cannot be overcome
   D. the solution of problems in supervision is best achieved by scientific methods

9._____

10. Suppose that a stenographer recently appointed to your bureau submits a memorandum suggesting a change in office procedure that has been tried before and has been found unsuccessful.
Of the following, the BEST action for you to take is to
   A. send the stenographer a note acknowledging receipt of the suggestion, but do not attempt to carry out the suggestion
   B. point out that suggestions should come from her supervisor, who has a better knowledge of the problems of the office
   C. try out the suggested change a second time, lest the stenographer lose interest in her work
   D. call the stenographer in, explain the change is not practicable, and compliment her for her interest and alertness

10._____

11. Suppose that you are an assistant to one of the important administrators in your department. You receive a note from the head of the department asking your superior to assist with a pressing problem that has arisen by making an immediate recommendation. Your superior is out of town on official business for a few days and cannot be reached. The head of the department, evidently, is not aware of his absence.
Of the following, the BEST action for you to take is
   A. send the note back to the head of the department without comment so as not to incriminate your supervisor
   B. forward the note to one of the administrators in another division of the department
   C. wait until your supervisor returns and bring the note to his attention immediately
   D. get in touch with the head of the department immediately and inform him that your superior is out of town

12. One of your duties may be to estimate the budget of your unit for the next fiscal year. Suppose that you expect no important changes in the work of your unit during the next year.
Of the following, the MOST appropriate basis for estimating next year's budget is the
   A. average budget of your unit for the last five years
   B. budget of your unit for the current year plus fifty percent to allow for possible expansion
   C. average current budget of units in your department
   D. budget of your unit for the current fiscal year

13. Suppose that you are acting as supervisor to an important administrator in your department. Of the following, the BEST reason for keeping a separate *pending* file of letters to which answers are expected very soon is that
   A. important correspondence should be placed in a separate, readily accessible file
   B. a periodic check of the *pending* file will indicate the possible need for follow-up letters
   C. correspondence is never final, so provision should be made for keeping files open
   D. there is seldom sufficient room in the permanent files to permit filing all letters

14. In order to BEST able to teach a newly appointed employee who must learn to do a type of work which is unfamiliar to him, his supervisor should realize that during the first stage in the learning process the subordinate is generally characterized by
   A. acute consciousness of self
   B. acute consciousness of subject matter, with little interest in persons or personalities
   C. inertness or passive acceptance of assigned role
   D. understanding of problems without understanding of the means of solving them

5 (#1)

15. The MOST accurate of the following principles of education and learning for a supervisor to keep in mind when planning a training program for the employees under his supervision is that

    A. his employees, like all other individuals, vary in the rate at which they learn new material and in the degree to which they can retain what they do learn
    B. experienced employees who have the same basic college education and agency experience will be able to learn new material at approximately the same rate of speed
    C. the speed with which employees can learn new material after the age of forty is half as rapid as at ages twenty to thirty
    D. with regard to any specific task, it is easier and takes less time to break an experienced employee of old, unsatisfactory work habits than it is to teach him new, acceptable ones

15._____

16. A supervisor has been transferred from supervision of one group of units to another group of units in the same center. He spends the first three weeks in his new assignment in getting acquainted with his new subordinates, their caseload problems, and their work. In this process, he notices that some of the case records and forms which are submitted to him by two of the assistant supervisors are carelessly or improperly prepared.
The BEST of the following actions for the supervisor to take in this situation is to

    A. carefully check the work submitted by these assistant supervisors during an additional three weeks before taking any more positive action
    B. confer with these offending workers and show each one where his work needs improvement and how to go about achieving it
    C. institute an in-service training program specifically designed to solve such a problem and instruct the entire subordinate staff in proper work methods
    D. make a note of these errors for documentary use in preparing the annual service rating reports and advise the workers involved to prepare their work more carefully

16._____

17. A supervisor, who was promoted to his position a year ago, has supervised a certain assistant supervisor for this one year. The work of the assistant supervisor has been very poor because he has done a minimum of work, refused to take sufficient responsibility, been difficult to handle, and required very close supervision. Apparently, due to the increasing insistency by his supervisor that he improve the caliber of his work, he assistant supervisor tenders his resignation, stating that the demands of the job are too much for him. The opinion of the previous supervisor, who had supervised this assistant supervisor for two years, agrees substantially with that of the new supervisor. Under such circumstances, the BEST of the following actions the supervisor can take in general is to

    A. recommend that the resignation be accepted and that he be rehired should he later apply when he feels able to do the job
    B. recommend that the resignation be accepted and that he not be rehired should he later so apply

17._____

C. refuse to accept the resignation but try to persuade the assistant supervisor to accept psychiatric help
D. refuse to accept the resignation, promising the assistant supervisor that he will be less closely supervised in the future since he is now so experienced

18. Rumors have arisen to the effect that one of the social investigators under your supervision has been attending classes at a local university during afternoon hours when he is supposed to be making field visits.
The BEST of the following ways for you to approach this problem is to
   A. disregard the rumors since, like most rumors, they probably have no actual foundation in fact
   B. have a discreet investigation made in order to determine the actual facts prior to taking any other action
   C. inform the investigator that you know what he has been doing and that such behavior is overt dereliction of duty and is punishable by dismissal
   D. review the investigator's work record, spot check his cases and take no further action unless the quality of his work is below average for the unit

19. The one of the following instances when it is MOST important for an upper level supervisor to follow the chain of command is when he is
   A. communicating decisions   B. communicating information
   C. receiving suggestions   D. seeking information

20. In order to maintain a proper relationship with a worker who is assigned to staff rather than line functions, a line supervisor should
   A. accept all recommendations of the staff worker
   B. include the staff worker in the conferences called by the supervisor for his subordinates
   C. keep the staff worker informed of developments in the area of his staff assignment
   D. require that the staff worker's recommendations be communicated to the supervisor through the supervisor's own superior

21. Of the following, the GREATEST disadvantage of placing a worker in a staff position under the direct supervision of the supervisor whom he advises is the possibility that the
   A. staff worker will tend to be insubordinate because of a feeling of superiority over the supervisor
   B. staff worker will tend to give advice of the type which the supervisor wants to hear or finds acceptable
   C. supervisor will tend to be mistrustful of the advice of a worker of subordinate rank
   D. supervisor will tend to derive little benefit from the advice because to supervise properly he should know at least as much as his subordinate

22. One factor which might be given consideration in deciding upon the optimum span of control of a supervisor over his immediate subordinates is the position of the supervisor in the hierarchy of the organization. It is generally considered PROPER that the number of subordinates immediately supervised by a higher, upper echelon supervisor
    A. is unrelated to and tends to form no pattern with the number supervised by lower level supervisors
    B. should be about the same as the number supervised by a lower level supervisor
    C. should be larger than the number supervised by a lower level supervisor
    D. should be smaller than the number supervised by a lower level supervisor

22.____

23. An important administrative problem is how precisely to define the limits on authority that are delegated to subordinate supervisors. Such definition of limits of authority should be
    A. as precise as possible and practicable in all areas
    B. as precise as possible and practicable in areas of function, but should allow considerable flexibility in the area of personnel management
    C. as precise as possible and practicable in the area of personnel management, but should allow considerable flexibility both in the areas of function and in the areas of personnel management
    D. in general terms so as to allow considerable flexibility both in the areas of function and in the areas of personnel management

23.____

24. The one of the following causes of clerical error which is usually considered to be LEAST attributable to faulty supervision or inefficient management is
    A. inability to carry out instructions
    B. too much work to do
    C. an inappropriate record-keeping system
    D. continual interruptions

24.____

25. Assume that you are the supervisor of a clerical unit in a large agency. One of your subordinates violates a rule of the agency, a violation which requires that the employee be suspended from his work for one day. The violated rule is one that you have found to be unduly strict and you have recommended to the management of the agency that the rule be changed or abolished. The management has been considering your recommendation but has not yet reached a decision on the matter.
In these circumstances, you should
    A. not initiate disciplinary action, but, instead, explain to the employee that the rule may be changed shortly
    B. delay disciplinary action on the violation until the management has reached a decision on changing the rule
    C. modify the disciplinary action by reprimanding the employee and informing him that further action may be taken when the management has reached a decision on changing the rule
    D. initiate the prescribed disciplinary action without commenting on the strictness of the rule or on your recommendation

25.____

KEY (CORRECT ANSWERS)

1.	C		11.	D
2.	C		12.	D
3.	D		13.	B
4.	A		14.	A
5.	C		15.	A
6.	C		16.	B
7.	C		17.	B
8.	B		18.	B
9.	B		19.	A
10.	D		20.	C

21. B
22. D
23. A
24. A
25. D

TEST 2

DIRECTIONS: Each question or incomplete statement is followed by several suggested answers or completions. Select the one that BEST answers the question or completes the statement. *PRINT THE LETTER OF THE CORRECT ANSWER IN THE SPACE AT THE RIGHT.*

1. As a supervisor, assume that a newly appointed employee is assigned to your unit.
   The one of the following which is likely to have the LEAST value in motivating the new employee when he first reports to you is
   A. an explanation of disciplinary measures which may be taken against employees
   B. indication by you that he can always come to you for help
   C. the first impression he gets of you and his fellow employees
   D. your emphasis on the importance of the work when interviewing him

   1.____

2. Assume that you are in charge of a unit of employees. A new appointee reports to you for the first time.
   Of the following, the MOST advisable action for you to take first is to
   A. attempt to evaluate his attitude towards the work he will be required to perform
   B. discuss with him the general nature of the duties he is to perform
   C. explain the opportunities he will have for promotion within the department
   D. have him read over any available material pertaining to departmental rules and regulations for employees

   2.____

3. Your department conducts a formal training course for new appointees.
   Under these circumstances, a supervisor should assume that
   A. he can safely delegate all responsibility for any additional training required to one of his experienced men who will work with the new appointee in the field
   B. he is thus relieved of the effort required to train new appointees who may be assigned to his unit
   C. he will still be responsible for supplementary training of new appointees assigned to his unit
   D. his responsibility for training should be limited to making suggestions for improving the formal training program based on his observation of the work of new appointees

   3.____

4. In the development of an on-the-job training program, the FIRST step should be
   A. consideration of the cost of such a program
   B. consideration of the problem of interesting the workers in such a program
   C. determination of the training facilities which may be available
   D. determination of those areas in which training is required

   4.____

5. Assume that a recent appointee has completed whatever basic training was provided for him. It becomes necessary to give him a special assignment for which he has not been specifically trained. He is given this assignment without any instructions as to how it should be carried out. This should be considered as
   A. *advisable*, because a worker has to feel his own way on special assignments
   B. *advisable*, because there comes a time when a worker should be encouraged to exercise his own initiative
   C. *inadvisable*, because a worker needs guidance on any aspect of the job with which he is unfamiliar
   D. *inadvisable*, because various superior officials of the department may have different ideas concerning the methods to be used in special assignments

6. Assume that you are holding a conference with the works in your unit. During the conference, one of the employees, in an offensive manner, challenges a statement you make. You are reasonably sure but not certain that what you have said is correct.
   The MOST advisable action for you to take at the conference is to
   A. admit that you may be in error but reprimand the man for his manner of speaking
   B. avail yourself of the opportunity to point out to the group what constitutes bad manners
   C. ignore the man's manner but make sure that the group feels your statement is correct
   D. say that you will determine the correct facts as soon as possible and inform the staff

7. Suppose that a new inspectional procedure has been ordered by the chief of your bureau. You think that it may meet with some objection by your staff.
   As a unit supervisor, the MOST advisable action for you to take in order to minimize such resistance is to
   A. appoint a committee from your staff to study the procedure and report on its advantages and disadvantages
   B. discuss, at a staff conference, the intent of the new procedure and the means of carrying it out
   C. inform the staff that this is an order coming from a higher authority and it must be carried out regardless of personal feelings
   D. issue detailed instructions concerning the new procedure to each member of your staff

8. Suppose that at conferences with your staff, you find that, usually, only one of the men participates in the discussion.
   Under these circumstances, the MOST advisable action for you to take is to
   A. speak to him privately and ask him to refrain from speaking so much at staff conferences
   B. stimulate the other men by asking them direct questions at staff conferences

3 (#2)

    C. tell him directly, at conferences, that you would prefer to hear from the other men for a change
    D. use the technique of not looking at this man when asking questions in order to prevent him from getting the floor

9. Which of the following do you consider to be the MOST important factor to be considered in evaluating the work of an employee. His 9.____
    A. ability to maintain good personal relationships with his supervisor, his fellow workers, and the community
    B. effectiveness in helping to carry out the objectives of the program
    C. observance of departmental rules and regulations governing employees
    D. personal awareness of the significance of his work to the welfare of the community

10. Of the following, the MOST valid statement concerning the supervisor and the probationary period is: 10.____
    A. Proper personnel selection methods should make it unnecessary for supervisory personnel to be concerned with evaluation of probationers
    B. Requiring an immediate supervisor to report on the capability of a candidate at the end of his probationary period is inadvisable since he usually has had no part in the initial selection of personnel
    C. The probationary period should be considered as an integral part of the personnel selection process and, thus, should be an active concern of immediate supervisors
    D. The value of a probationary period is likely to be greater when the supervisor is required to report only when he considers a candidate not suitable for permanent appointment rather when he is required to certify that a candidate is suitable

11. An employee under your supervision complains to you about the fact that you recommended him for a performance rating indicating merely satisfactory work. He feels that he deserves a higher rating, while you are convinced that your recommendation was justified.
Of the following, the MOST advisable action for you to take is to 11.____
    A. advise him of his right to appeal the rating given and the required procedure for making such an appeal
    B. explain to him that, as a supervisor, your experience and your opportunity to evaluate his work against that of other employees enable you to give him a fair and just rating
    C. give him your specific reasons for considering his performance average or satisfactory and not qualifying for a higher rating
    D. point out to him that relatively few persons receive an above-average rating and that there is always opportunity for a higher rating in the future

12. Assume that your superior has assigned to your unit a special investigation which is to be completed by a certain date. Considering the regular work load, you feel that the investigation cannot be completed in the allotted time. You point this out to him but he insists that you handle the assignment without any increase in staff.
Of the following, the MOST advisable course of action for you to take is to
    A. agree to undertake the assignment but insist upon some assurance that this situation will not be repeated
    B. be as noncommittal as possible with the determination to secure evidence to show that you should not be given the assignment
    C. take the matter up with higher authority but inform him that you have done so
    D. undertake the assignment with the intention to keep him closely informed concerning the progress of the work

13. Assume that, as a supervisor, you have received somewhat conflicting orders from two superiors not of equal rank.
Of the following, the MOST advisable course of action for you to follow is to
    A. attempt to carry out the orders of each superior as far as you can
    B. carry out the orders of the person higher in rank
    C. consult your immediate superior concerning the situation
    D. use your own judgment and follow those orders which seem more reasonable

14. Assume that you are a supervisor. Your immediate superior frequently gives assignments to your subordinates without your knowledge.
Of the following, the MOST advisable way for you to handle this situation is to
    A. discuss it with your immediate supervisor
    B. instruct your staff that they are to accept assignments only from you
    C. keep a record of such instances and forward a memorandum concerning them to higher authority in the department
    D. realize and accept the fact that, as your superior, he has authority over you

15. Of the following, the one which would LEAST likely aid a supervisor in long-range planning is
    A. a practical attitude of not worrying about possible problems until they arise
    B. estimating future needs on the basis of past experience
    C. obtaining early knowledge of contemplated changes
    D. staff conferences with the employees under his supervision

16. Of the following, the one that is likely to be of LEAST value as a direct source of help for a supervisor is
    A. a compilation of departmental rules and regulations
    B. a manual of standard operating procedures
    C. civil service rules and regulations
    D. the personnel officer of the department

17. Assume that you suspect that a field worker under your supervision goes home early in the afternoon. In spotchecking one of his daily reports, you find that he has indicated that his last inspection was made at a certain establishment at 4 P.M. The owner of the establishment states that the inspection was made at 1 P.M.
Of the following, the MOST advisable course of action for you to take FIRST is to
    A. attempt to determine whether any animosity exists between the owner of this establishment and the employee
    B. check with owners of establishments listed on the report as having been visited before the establishment in question was visited
    C. confront the employee with the information you have obtained from the owner of the establishment
    D. send a report of these circumstances to your immediate supervisor

17._____

18. Assume that one of the employees under your supervision is frequently absent. Although you have discussed the matter with him several times, his attendance record remains unsatisfactory.
The MOST advisable course of action for you to take NEXT is to
    A. discuss the problem again with the employee to see if any new factors have arisen which cause his continued absence
    B. give him another chance
    C. recommend that appropriate penalties be applied since the problem has already been discussed with him
    D. advise him to seek expert counsel concerning his personal problems

18._____

19. Assume that you are a supervisor. One of the men you supervise angrily demands an interview with you to discuss his dissatisfaction with his work assignment.
Of the following, the course of action you should take FIRST in this situation is to
    A. advise him to take the matter up with your superior
    B. arrange for a private interview as soon as possible to discuss his grievance
    C. explain to the employee that all assignments are made by you only after consideration of what is best for satisfactory accomplishment of the work of the unit
    D. promise the employee that you will review the work assignments in your unit to determine whether any changes are warranted

19._____

20. Of the following, the one which would likely aid a supervisor MOST in maintaining morale among his staff is
    A. ignoring any rumors that are transmitted through the organization's grapevine
    B. maintenance of an aloof attitude in his contacts with the group under his supervision

20._____

6 (#2)

    C. scrupulous care in not revealing any information which the administration requests him to treat as confidential
    D. seeking, through consultation with his own superior, to find a remedy if situations outside of his division threaten to upset his own group

21. Of the following, the one which a supervisor should try to avoid MOST is 21.____
    A. consideration that rumors in the organization may contain some elements of truth
    B. handling of grievances which are voiced by his entire staff, as opposed to individual grievances
    C. offering personal counsel when it is requested of him by subordinates
    D. use of disciplinary measures to secure proper conduct of subordinates

22. Suppose that you are a supervisor. At a social function which you attend, unfavorable remarks concerning certain activities of our department are made in the course of conversation. You happen to be in agreement with what is being said. 22.____
Under these circumstances, you should consider that
    A. it is best to be noncommittal in such situations
    B. it is necessary for you to convince the others of the value of these activities
    C. it would be advisable for you to suggest that those interested write a group letter of complaint to the department
    D. you are a private citizen as well as a public employee and, therefore, are free to express your personal opinion at a social function

23. Assume that you are a supervisor in charge of an inspectional unit. A merchant whose weighing and measuring devices were tested by one of the inspectors under your supervision takes the trouble to write a letter of complaint to the Commissioner of the department. In this letter he states that the manner in which the inspection was conducted gave customers in the store the impression that improper devices were being used although no violations were found. The letter is referred to you for appropriate action. 23.____
Of the following, the MOST advisable action for you to take FIRST is to
    A. arrange for an inspector not known by the accused inspector to observe him in the field and report his findings to you
    B. call a staff meeting at which you will discuss proper procedures to be used when making inspections
    C. interview the inspector involved to get his version of the incident
    D. make personal observations, in the field, of the manner in which inspections are being conducted

24. In attempting to protect consumers against various types of fraud, the law states that, in certain instances, possession of a certain substance by a dealer is presumptive evidence of his intent to use it to defraud. 24.____
From the point of view of the enforcing agency, the PRINCIPAL value of such legislation is that
    A. it offers more protection of the rights of the consumer than it does of the rights of the dealer

B. such evidence, by its very nature, is superior to direct evidence
C. the agency is relieved of the difficulties involved in attempting to obtain direct evidence
D. this constitutes a more comprehensive definition of the offense involved

25. Departments of municipal government frequently suggest the enactment of legislation in fields in which they are interested.
Such suggestions are
    A. *advisable*, because basic legislation is already available
    B. *advisable*, because the departments have the best knowledge of their problems and needs
    C. *inadvisable*, because the city already has a Law Department
    D. *inadvisable*, because departments have biased viewpoints

25.____

KEY (CORRECT ANSWERS)

1.	A	11.	C
2.	B	12.	D
3.	C	13.	C
4.	D	14.	A
5.	C	15.	A
6.	D	16.	C
7.	B	17.	B
8.	B	18.	C
9.	B	19.	B
10.	C	20.	D

21.	D
22.	A
23.	C
24.	C
25.	B

PHILOSOPHY, PRINCIPLES, PRACTICES, AND TECHNICS
OF
SUPERVISION, ADMINISTRATION, MANAGEMENT, AND ORGANIZATION

TABLE OF CONTENTS

	Page
MEANING OF SUPERVISION	1
THE OLD AND THE NEW SUPERVISION	1
THE EIGHT (8) BASIC PRINCIPLES OF THE NEW SUPERVISION	1
I. Principle of Responsibility	1
II. Principle of Authority	2
III. Principle of Self-Growth	2
IV. Principle of Individual Worth	2
V. Principle of Creative Leadership	2
VI. Principle of Success and Failure	2
VII. Principle of Science	3
VIII. Principle of Cooperation	3
WHAT IS ADMINISTRATION?	3
I. Practices Commonly Classed as "Supervisory"	3
II. Practices Commonly Classed as "Administrative"	3
III. Practices Commonly Classed as Both "Supervisory" and "Administrative"	4
RESPONSIBILITIES OF THE SUPERVISOR	4
COMPETENCIES OF THE SUPERVISOR	4
THE PROFESSIONAL SUPERVISOR-EMPLOYEE RELATIONSHIP	4
MINI-TEXT IN SUPERVISION, ADMINISTRATION, MANAGEMENT, AND ORGANIZATION	5
I. Brief Highlights	5
A. Levels of Management	6
B. What the Supervisor Must Learn	6
C. A Definition of Supervision	6
D. Elements of the Team Concept	6
E. Principles of Organization	6
F. The Four Important Parts of Every Job	7
G. Principles of Delegation	7
H. Principles of Effective Communications	7
I. Principles of Work Improvement	7
J. Areas of Job Improvement	7
K. Seven Key Points in Making Improvements	8

	L.	Corrective Techniques for Job Improvement	8
	M.	A Planning Checklist	8
	N.	Five Characteristics of Good Directions	9
	O.	Types of Directions	9
	P.	Controls	9
	Q.	Orienting the New Employee	9
	R.	Checklist for Orienting New Employees	9
	S.	Principles of Learning	10
	T.	Causes of Poor Performance	10
	U.	Four Major Steps in On-the-Job Instructions	10
	V.	Employees Want Five Things	10
	W.	Some Don'ts in Regard to Praise	11
	X.	How to Gain Your Workers' Confidence	11
	Y.	Sources of Employee Problems	11
	Z.	The Supervisor's Key to Discipline	11
	AA.	Five Important Processes of Management	12
	BB.	When the Supervisor Fails to Plan	12
	CC.	Fourteen General Principles of Management	12
	DD.	Change	12
II.	Brief Topical Summaries		13
	A.	Who/What is the Supervisor?	13
	B.	The Sociology of Work	13
	C.	Principles and Practices of Supervision	14
	D.	Dynamic Leadership	14
	E.	Processes for Solving Problems	15
	F.	Training for Results	15
	G.	Health, Safety, and Accident Prevention	16
	H.	Equal Employment Opportunity	16
	I.	Improving Communications	16
	J.	Self-Development	17
	K.	Teaching and Training	17
		1. The Teaching Process	17
		a. Preparation	17
		b. Presentation	18
		c. Summary	18
		d. Application	18
		e. Evaluation	18
		2. Teaching Methods	18
		a. Lecture	18
		b. Discussion	18
		c. Demonstration	19
		d. Performance	19
		e. Which Method to Use	19

PHILOSOPHY, PRINCIPLES, PRACTICES, AND TECHNICS OF SUPERVISION, ADMINISTRATION, MANAGEMENT, AND ORGANIZATION

MEANING OF SUPERVISION

The extension of the democratic philosophy has been accompanied by an extension in the scope of supervision. Modern leaders and supervisors no longer think of supervision in the narrow sense of being confined chiefly to visiting employees, supplying materials, or rating the staff. They regard supervision as being intimately related to all the concerned agencies of society, they speak of the supervisor's function in terms of "growth," rather than the "improvement" of employees.

This modern concept of supervision may be defined as follows: Supervision is leadership and the development of leadership within groups which are cooperatively engaged in inspection, research, training, guidance, and evaluation.

THE OLD AND THE NEW SUPERVISION

TRADITIONAL
1. Inspection
2. Focused on the employee
3. Visitation
4. Random and haphazard
5. Imposed and authoritarian
6. One person usually

MODERN
1. Study and analysis
2. Focused on aims, materials, methods, supervisors, employees, environment
3. Demonstrations, intervisitation, workshops, directed reading, bulletins, etc.
4. Definitely organized and planned (scientific)
5. Cooperative and democratic
6. Many persons involved (creative)

THE EIGHT (8) BASIC PRINCIPLES OF THE NEW SUPERVISION

I. Principle of Responsibility
   Authority to act and responsibility for acting must be joined.
   A. If you give responsibility, give authority.
   B. Define employee duties clearly.
   C. Protect employees from criticism by others.
   D. Recognize the rights as well as obligations of employees.
   E. Achieve the aims of a democratic society insofar as it is possible within the area of your work.
   F. Establish a situation favorable to training and learning.
   G. Accept ultimate responsibility for everything done in your section, unit, office, division, department.
   H. Good administration and good supervision are inseparable.

II. Principle of Authority
The success of the supervisor is measured by the extent to which the power of authority is not used.
   A. Exercise simplicity and informality in supervision
   B. Use the simplest machinery of supervision
   C. If it is good for the organization as a whole, it is probably justified.
   D. Seldom be arbitrary or authoritative.
   E. Do not base your work on the power of position or of personality.
   F. Permit and encourage the free expression of opinions.

III. Principle of Self-Growth
The success of the supervisor is measured by the extent to which, and the speed with which, he is no longer needed.
   A. Base criticism on principles, not on specifics.
   B. Point out higher activities to employees.
   C. Train for self-thinking by employees to meet new situations.
   D. Stimulate initiative, self-reliance, and individual responsibility
   E. Concentrate on stimulating the growth of employees rather than on removing defects.

IV. Principle of Individual Worth
Respect for the individual is a paramount consideration in supervision.
   A. Be human and sympathetic in dealing with employees.
   B. Don't nag about things to be done.
   C. Recognize the individual differences among employees and seek opportunities to permit best expression of each personality.

V. Principle of Creative Leadership
The best supervision is that which is not apparent to the employee.
   A. Stimulate, don't drive employees to creative action.
   B. Emphasize doing good things.
   C. Encourage employees to do what they do best.
   D. Do not be too greatly concerned with details of subject or method.
   E. Do not be concerned exclusively with immediate problems and activities.
   F. Reveal higher activities and make them both desired and maximally possible.
   G. Determine procedures in the light of each situation but see that these are derived from a sound basic philosophy.
   H. Aid, inspire, and lead so as to liberate the creative spirit latent in all good employees.

VI. Principle of Success and Failure
There are no unsuccessful employees, only unsuccessful supervisors who have failed to give proper leadership.
   A. Adapt suggestions to the capacities, attitudes, and prejudices of employees.
   B. Be gradual, be progressive, be persistent.
   C. Help the employee find the general principle; have the employee apply his own problem to the general principle.
   D. Give adequate appreciation for good work and honest effort.
   E. Anticipate employee difficulties and help to prevent them.
   F. Encourage employees to do the desirable things they will do anyway.
   G. Judge your supervision by the results it secures.

VII. Principle of Science
Successful supervision is scientific, objective, and experimental. It is based on facts, not on prejudices.
    A. Be cumulative in results.
    B. Never divorce your suggestions from the goals of training.
    C. Don't be impatient of results.
    D. Keep all matters on a professional, not a personal, level.
    E. Do not be concerned exclusively with immediate problems and activities.
    F. Use objective means of determining achievement and rating where possible.

VIII. Principle of Cooperation
Supervision is a cooperative enterprise between supervisor and employee.
    A. Begin with conditions as they are.
    B. Ask opinions of all involved when formulating policies.
    C. Organization is as good as its weakest link.
    D. Let employees help to determine policies and department programs.
    E. Be approachable and accessible—physically and mentally.
    F. Develop pleasant social relationships.

WHAT IS ADMINISTRATION

Administration is concerned with providing the environment, the material facilities, and the operational procedures that will promote the maximum growth and development of supervisors and employees. (Organization is an aspect and a concomitant of administration.)

There is no sharp line of demarcation between supervision and administration; these functions are intimately interrelated and, often, overlapping. They are complementary activities.

I. Practices Commonly Classed as "Supervisory"
    A. Conducting employees' conferences
    B. Visiting sections, units, offices, divisions, departments
    C. Arranging for demonstrations
    D. Examining plans
    E. Suggesting professional reading
    F. Interpreting bulletins
    G. Recommending in-service training courses
    H. Encouraging experimentation
    I. Appraising employee morale
    J. Providing for intervisitation

II. Practices Commonly Classified as "Administrative"
    A. Management of the office
    B. Arrangement of schedules for extra duties
    C. Assignment of rooms or areas
    D. Distribution of supplies
    E. Keeping records and reports
    F. Care of audio-visual materials
    G. Keeping inventory records
    H. Checking record cards and books

  I. Programming special activities
  J. Checking on the attendance and punctuality of employees

III. Practices Commonly Classified as Both "Supervisory" and "Administrative"
  A. Program construction
  B. Testing or evaluating outcomes
  C. Personnel accounting
  D. Ordering instructional materials

RESPONSIBILITIES OF THE SUPERVISOR

A person employed in a supervisory capacity must constantly be able to improve his own efficiency and ability. He represent the employer to the employees and only continuous self-examination can make him a capable supervisor.

Leadership and training are the supervisor's responsibility. An efficient working unit is one in which the employees work with the supervisor. It is his job to bring out the best in his employees. He must always be relaxed, courteous, and calm in his association with his employees. Their feelings are important, and a harsh attitude does not develop the most efficient employees.

COMPETENCES OF THE SUPERVISOR

  I. Complete knowledge of the duties and responsibilities of his position.
  II. To be able to organize a job, plan ahead, and carry through.
  III. To have self-confidence and initiative.
  IV. To be able to handle the unexpected situation and make quick decisions.
  V. To be able to properly train subordinates in the positions they are best suited for.
  VI. To be able to keep good human relations among his subordinates.
  VII. To be able to keep good human relations between his subordinates and himself and to earn their respect and trust.

THE PROFESSIONAL SUPERVISOR-EMPLOYEE RELATIONSHIP

There are two kinds of efficiency: one kind is only apparent and is produced in organizations through the exercise of mere discipline; this is but a simulation of the second, or true, efficiency which springs from spontaneous cooperation. If you are a manager, no matter how great or small your responsibility, it is your job, in the final analysis, to create and develop this involuntary cooperation among the people whom you supervise. For, no matter how powerful a combination of money, machines, and materials a company may have, this is a dead and sterile thing without a team of willing, thinking, and articulate people to guide it.

The following 21 points are presented as indicative of the exemplary basic relationship that should exist between supervisor and employee:

1. Each person wants to be liked and respected by his fellow employee and wants to be treated with consideration and respect by his superior.
2. The most competent employee will make an error. However, in a unit where good relations exist between the supervisor and his employees, tenseness and fear do not exist. Thus, errors are not hidden or covered up, and the efficiency of a unit is not impaired.

3. Subordinates resent rules, regulations, or orders that are unreasonable or unexplained.
4. Subordinates are quick to resent unfairness, harshness, injustices, and favoritism.
5. An employee will accept responsibility if he knows that he will be complimented for a job well done, and not too harshly chastised for failure; that his supervisor will check the cause of the failure, and, if it was the supervisor's fault, he will assume the blame therefore. If it was the employee's fault, his supervisor will explain the correct method or means of handling the responsibility.
6. An employee wants to receive credit for a suggestion he has made, that is used. If a suggestion cannot be used, the employee is entitled to an explanation. The supervisor should not say "no" and close the subject.
7. Fear and worry slow up a worker's ability. Poor working environment can impair his physical and mental health. A good supervisor avoids forceful methods, threats, and arguments to get a job done.
8. A forceful supervisor is able to train his employees individually and as a team, and is able to motivate them in the proper channels.
9. A mature supervisor is able to properly evaluate his subordinates and to keep them happy and satisfied.
10. A sensitive supervisor will never patronize his subordinates.
11. A worthy supervisor will respect his employees' confidences.
12. Definite and clear-cut responsibilities should be assigned to each executive.
13. Responsibility should always be coupled with corresponding authority.
14. No change should be made in the scope or responsibilities of a position without a definite understanding to that effect on the part of all persons concerned.
15. No executive or employee, occupying a single position in the organization, should be subject to definite orders from more than one source.
16. Orders should never be given to subordinates over the head of a responsible executive. Rather than do this, the officer in question should be supplanted.
17. Criticisms of subordinates should, whoever possible, be made privately, and in no case should a subordinate be criticized in the presence of executives or employees of equal or lower rank.
18. No dispute or difference between executives or employees as to authority or responsibilities should be considered too trivial for prompt and careful adjudication.
19. Promotions, wage changes, and disciplinary action should always be approved by the executive immediately superior to the one directly responsible.
20. No executive or employee should ever be required, or expected, to be at the same time an assistant to, and critic of, another.
21. Any executive whose work is subject to regular inspection should, wherever practicable, be given the assistance and facilities necessary to enable him to maintain an independent check of the quality of his work.

MINI-TEXT IN SUPERVISION, ADMINISTRATION, MANAGEMENT, AND ORGANIZATION

I. Brief Highlights

Listed concisely and sequentially are major headings and important data in the field for quick recall and review.

A. Levels of Management
Any organization of some size has several levels of management. In terms of a ladder, the levels are:

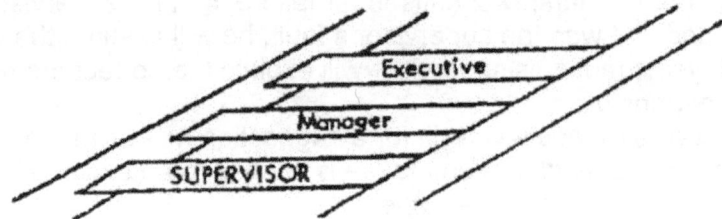

The first level is very important because it is the beginning point of management leadership.

B. What the Supervisor Must Learn
A supervisor must learn to:
1. Deal with people and their differences
2. Get the job done through people
3. Recognize the problems when they exist
4. Overcome obstacles to good performance
5. Evaluate the performance of people
6. Check his own performance in terms of accomplishment

C. A Definition of Supervisor
The term supervisor means any individual having authority, in the interests of the employer, to hire, transfer, suspend, lay-off, recall, promote, discharge, assign, reward, or discipline other employees or responsibility to direct them, or to adjust their grievances, or effectively to recommend such action, if, in connection with the foregoing, exercise of such authority is not of a merely routine or clerical nature but requires the use of independent judgment.

D. Elements of the Team Concept
What is involved in teamwork? The component parts are:
1. Members
2. A leader
3. Goals
4. Plans
5. Cooperation
6. Spirit

E. Principles of Organization
1. A team member must know what his job is.
2. Be sure that the nature and scope of a job are understood.
3. Authority and responsibility should be carefully spelled out.
4. A supervisor should be permitted to make the maximum number of decisions affecting his employees.
5. Employees should report to only one supervisor.
6. A supervisor should direct only as many employees as he can handle effectively.
7. An organization plan should be flexible.

8. Inspection and performance of work should be separate.
9. Organizational problems should receive immediate attention.
10. Assign work in line with ability and experience.

F. The Four Important Parts of Every Job
1. Inherent in every job is the *accountability* for results.
2. A second set of factors in every job is *responsibilities*.
3. Along with duties and responsibilities one must have the *authority* to act within certain limits without obtaining permission to proceed.
4. No job exists in a vacuum. The supervisor is surrounded by key *relationships*.

G. Principles of Delegation
Where work is delegated for the first time, the supervisor should think in terms of these questions:
1. Who is best qualified to do this?
2. Can an employee improve his abilities by doing this?
3. How long should an employee spend on this?
4. Are there any special problems for which he will need guidance?
5. How broad a delegation can I make?

H. Principles of Effective Communications
1. Determine the media.
2. To whom directed?
3. Identification and source authority.
4. Is communication understood?

I. Principles of Work Improvement
1. Most people usually do only the work which is assigned to them.
2. Workers are likely to fit assigned work into the time available to perform it.
3. A good workload usually stimulates output.
4. People usually do their best work when they know that results will be reviewed or inspected.
5. Employees usually feel that someone else is responsible for conditions of work, workplace layout, job methods, type of tools/equipment, and other such factors.
6. Employees are usually defensive about their job security.
7. Employees have natural resistance to change.
8. Employees can support or destroy a supervisor.
9. A supervisor usually earns the respect of his people through his personal example of diligence and efficiency.

J. Areas of Job Improvement
The areas of job improvement are quite numerous, but the most common ones which a supervisor can identify and utilize are:
1. Departmental layout
2. Flow of work
3. Workplace layout
4. Utilization of manpower
5. Work methods
6. Materials handling

7. Utilization
8. Motion economy

K. Seven Key Points in Making Improvements
1. Select the job to be improved
2. Study how it is being done now
3. Question the present method
4. Determine actions to be taken
5. Chart proposed method
6. Get approval and apply
7. Solicit worker participation

l. Corrective Techniques of Job Improvement
Specific Problems
1. Size of workload
2. Inability to meet schedules
3. Strain and fatigue
4. Improper use of men and skills
5. Waste, poor quality, unsafe conditions
6. Bottleneck conditions that hinder output
7. Poor utilization of equipment and machine
8. Efficiency and productivity of labor

General Improvement
1. Departmental layout
2. Flow of work
3. Work plan layout
4. Utilization of manpower
5. Work methods
6. Materials handling
7. Utilization of equipment
8. Motion economy

Corrective Techniques
1. Study with scale model
2. Flow chart study
3. Motion analysis
4. Comparison of units produced to standard allowance
5. Methods analysis
6. Flow chart and equipment study
7. Down time vs. running time
8. Motion analysis

M. A Planning Checklist
1. Objectives
2. Controls
3. Delegations
4. Communications
5. Resources
6. Manpower

7. Equipment
8. Supplies and materials
9. Utilization of time
10. Safety
11. Money
12. Work
13. Timing of improvements

N. Five Characteristics of Good Directions
In order to get results, directions must be:
1. Possible of accomplishment
2. Agreeable with worker interests
3. Related to mission
4. Planned and complete
5. Unmistakably clear

O. Types of Directions
1. Demands or direct orders
2. Requests
3. Suggestion or implication
4. volunteering

P. Controls
A typical listing of the overall areas in which the supervisor should establish controls might be:
1. Manpower
2. Materials
3. Quality of work
4. Quantity of work
5. Time
6. Space
7. Money
8. Methods

Q. Orienting the New Employee
1. Prepare for him
2. Welcome the new employee
3. Orientation for the job
4. Follow-up

R. Checklist for Orienting New Employees   Yes   No
1. Do you appreciate the feelings of new employees
   when they first report for work?   ___   ___
2. Are you aware of the fact that the new employee must
   make a big adjustment to his job?   ___   ___
3. Have you given him good reasons for liking the job and
   the organization?   ___   ___
4. Have you prepared for his first day on the job?   ___   ___
5. Did you welcome him cordially and make him feel needed? ___   ___

                                                                    Yes   No

    6. Did you establish rapport with him so that he feels free
        to talk and discuss matters with you?   ___   ___
    7. Did you explain his job to him and his relationship to you? ___   ___
    8. Does he know that his work will be evaluated periodically
        on a basis that is fair and objective?   ___   ___
    9. Did you introduce him to his fellow workers in such a way
        that they are likely to accept him?   ___   ___
    10. Does he know what employee benefits he will receive?   ___   ___
    11. Does he understand the importance of being on the job
        and what to do if he must leave his duty station?   ___   ___
    12. Has he been impressed with the importance of accident
        prevention and safe practice?   ___   ___
    13. Does he generally know his way around the department?   ___   ___
    14. Is he under the guidance of a sponsor who will teach
        the right way of doing things?   ___   ___
    15. Do you plan to follow-up so that he will continue to adjust
        successfully to his job?   ___   ___

S. Principles of Learning
    1. Motivation
    2. Demonstration or explanation
    3. Practice

T. Causes of Poor Performance
    1. Improper training for job
    2. Wrong tools
    3. Inadequate directions
    4. Lack of supervisory follow-up
    5. Poor communications
    6. Lack of standards of performance
    7. Wrong work habits
    8. Low morale
    9. Other

U. Four Major Steps in On-The-Job Instruction
    1. Prepare the worker
    2. Present the operation
    3. Tryout performance
    4. Follow-up

V. Employees Want Five Things
    1. Security
    2. Opportunity
    3. Recognition
    4. Inclusion
    5. Expression

W. Some Don'ts in Regard to Praise
1. Don't praise a person for something he hasn't done.
2. Don't praise a person unless you can be sincere.
3. Don't be sparing in praise just because your superior withholds it from you.
4. Don't let too much time elapse between good performance and recognition of it

X. How to Gain Your Workers' Confidence
Methods of developing confidence include such things as:
1. Knowing the interests, habits, hobbies of employees
2. Admitting your own inadequacies
3. Sharing and telling of confidence in others
4. Supporting people when they are in trouble
5. Delegating matters that can be well handled
6. Being frank and straightforward about problems and working conditions
7. Encouraging others to bring their problems to you
8. Taking action on problems which impede worker progress

Y. Sources of Employee Problems
On-the-job causes might be such things as:
1. A feeling that favoritism is exercised in assignments
2. Assignment of overtime
3. An undue amount of supervision
4. Changing methods or systems
5. Stealing of ideas or trade secrets
6. Lack of interest in job
7. Threat of reduction in force
8. Ignorance or lack of communications
9. Poor equipment
10. Lack of knowing how supervisor feels toward employee
11. Shift assignments

Off-the-job problems might have to do with:
1. Health
2. Finances
3. Housing
4. Family

Z. The Supervisor's Key to Discipline
There are several key points about discipline which the supervisor should keep in mind:
1. Job discipline is one of the disciplines of life and is directed by the supervisor.
2. It is more important to correct an employee fault than to fix blame for it.
3. Employee performance is affected by problems both on the job and off.
4. Sudden or abrupt changes in behavior can be indications of important employee problems.
5. Problems should be dealt with as soon as possible after they are identified.
6. The attitude of the supervisor may have more to do with solving problems than the techniques of problem solving.
7. Correction of employee behavior should be resorted to only after the supervisor is sure that training or counseling will not be helpful.

8. Be sure to document your disciplinary actions.
9. Make sure that you are disciplining on the basis of facts rather than personal feelings.
10. Take each disciplinary step in order, being careful not to make snap judgments, or decisions based on impatience.

AA. Five Important Processes of Management
1. Planning
2. Organizing
3. Scheduling
4. Controlling
5. Motivating

BB. When the Supervisor Fails to Plan
1. Supervisor creates impression of not knowing his job
2. May lead to excessive overtime
3. Job runs itself—supervisor lacks control
4. Deadlines and appointments missed
5. Parts of the work go undone
6. Work interrupted by emergencies
7. Sets a bad example
8. Uneven workload creates peaks and valleys
9. Too much time on minor details at expense of more important tasks

CC. Fourteen General Principles of Management
1. Division of work
2. Authority and responsibility
3. Discipline
4. Unity of command
5. Unity of direction
6. Subordination of individual interest to general interest
7. Remuneration of personnel
8. Centralization
9. Scalar chain
10. Order
11. Equity
12. Stability of tenure of personnel
13. Initiative
14. Esprit de corps

DD. Change

Bringing about change is perhaps attempted more often, and yet less well understood, than anything else the supervisor does. How do people generally react to change? (People tend to resist change that is imposed upon them by other individuals or circumstances.

Change is characteristic of every situation. It is a part of every real endeavor where the efforts of people are concerned.

13

1. Why do people resist change?
   People may resist change because of:
   a. Fear of the unknown
   b. Implied criticism
   c. Unpleasant experiences in the past
   d. Fear of loss of status
   e. Threat to the ego
   f. Fear of loss of economic stability

2. How can we best overcome the resistance to change?
   In initiating change, take these steps:
   a. Get ready to sell
   b. Identify sources of help
   c. Anticipate objections
   d. Sell benefits
   e. Listen in depth
   f. Follow up

II. Brief Topical Summaries

   A. Who/What is the Supervisor?
      1. The supervisor is often called the "highest level employee and the lowest level manager."
      2. A supervisor is a member of both management and the work group. He acts as a bridge between the two.
      3. Most problems in supervision are in the area of human relations, or people problems.
      4. Employees expect: Respect, opportunity to learn and to advance, and a sense of belonging, and so forth.
      5. Supervisors are responsible for directing people and organizing work. Planning is of paramount importance.
      6. A position description is a set of duties and responsibilities inherent to a given position.
      7. It is important to keep the position description up-to-date and to provide each employee with his own copy.

   B. The Sociology of Work
      1. People are alike in many ways; however, each individual is unique.
      2. The supervisor is challenged in getting to know employee differences. Acquiring skills in evaluating individuals is an asset.
      3. Maintaining meaningful working relationships in the organization is of great importance.
      4. The supervisor has an obligation to help individuals to develop to their fullest potential.
      5. Job rotation on a planned basis helps to build versatility and to maintain interest and enthusiasm in work groups.
      6. Cross training (job rotation) provides backup skills.

7. The supervisor can help reduce tension by maintaining a sense of humor, providing guidance to employees, and by making reasonable and timely decisions. Employees respond favorably to working under reasonably predictable circumstances.
8. Change is characteristic of all managerial behavior. The supervisor must adjust to changes in procedures, new methods, technological changes, and to a number of new and sometimes challenging situations.
9. To overcome the natural tendency for people to resist change, the supervisor should become more skillful in initiating change.

C. Principles and Practices of Supervision
1. Employees should be required to answer to only one superior.
2. A supervisor can effectively direct only a limited number of employees, depending upon the complexity, variety, and proximity of the jobs involved.
3. The organizational chart presents the organization in graphic form. It reflects lines of authority and responsibility as well as interrelationships of units within the organization.
4. Distribution of work can be improved through an analysis using the "Work Distribution Chart."
5. The "Work Distribution Chart" reflects the division of work within a unit in understandable form.
6. When related tasks are given to an employee, he has a better chance of increasing his skills through training.
7. The individual who is given the responsibility for tasks must also be given the appropriate authority to insure adequate results.
8. The supervisor should delegate repetitive, routine work. Preparation of recurring reports, maintaining leave and attendance records are some examples.
9. Good discipline is essential to good task performance. Discipline is reflected in the actions of employees on the job in the absence of supervision.
10. Disciplinary action may have to be taken when the positive aspects of discipline have failed. Reprimand, warning, and suspension are examples of disciplinary action.
11. If a situation calls for a reprimand, be sure it is deserved and remember it is to be done in private.

D. Dynamic Leadership
1. A style is a personal method or manner of exerting influence.
2. Authoritarian leaders often see themselves as the source of power and authority.
3. The democratic leader often perceives the group as the source of authority and power.
4. Supervisors tend to do better when using the pattern of leadership that is most natural for them.
5. Social scientists suggest that the effective supervisor use the leadership style that best fits the problem or circumstances involved.
6. All four styles—telling, selling, consulting, joining—have their place. Using one does not preclude using the other at another time.

7. The theory X point of view assumes that the average person dislikes work, will avoid it whenever possible, and must be coerced to achieve organizational objectives.
8. The theory Y point of view assumes that the average person considers work to be a natural as play, and, when the individual is committed, he requires little supervision or direction to accomplish desired objectives.
9. The leader's basic assumptions concerning human behavior and human nature affect his actions, decisions, and other managerial practices.
10. Dissatisfaction among employees is often present, but difficult to isolate. The supervisor should seek to weaken dissatisfaction by keeping promises, being sincere and considerate, keeping employees informed, and so forth.
11. Constructive suggestions should be encouraged during the natural progress of the work.

E. Processes for Solving Problems
1. People find their daily tasks more meaningful and satisfying when they can improve them.
2. The causes of problems, or the key factors, are often hidden in the background. Ability to solve problems often involves the ability to isolate them from their backgrounds. There is some substance to the cliché that some persons "can't see the forest for the trees."
3. New procedures are often developed from old ones. Problems should be broken down into manageable parts. New ideas can be adapted from old one.
4. People think differently in problem-solving situations. Using a logical, patterned approach is often useful. One approach found to be useful includes these steps:
   a. Define the problem
   b. Establish objectives
   c. Get the facts
   d. Weigh and decide
   e. Take action
   f. Evaluate action

F. Training for Results
1. Participants respond best when they feel training is important to them.
2. The supervisor has responsibility for the training and development of those who report to him.
3. When training is delegated to others, great care must be exercised to insure the trainer has knowledge, aptitude, and interest for his work as a trainer.
4. Training (learning) of some type goes on continually. The most successful supervisor makes certain the learning contributes in a productive manner to operational goals.
5. New employees are particularly susceptible to training. Older employees facing new job situations require specific training, as well as having need for development and growth opportunities.
6. Training needs require continuous monitoring.
7. The training officer of an agency is a professional with a responsibility to assist supervisors in solving training problems.

8. Many of the self-development steps important to the supervisor's own growth are equally important to the development of peers and subordinates. Knowledge of these is important when the supervisor consults with others on development and growth opportunities.

G. Health, Safety, and Accident Prevention
1. Management-minded supervisors take appropriate measures to assist employees in maintaining health and in assuring safe practices in the work environment.
2. Effective safety training and practices help to avoid injury and accidents.
3. Safety should be a management goal. All infractions of safety which are observed should be corrected without exception.
4. Employees' safety attitude, training and instruction, provision of safe tools and equipment, supervision, and leadership are considered highly important factors which contribute to safety and which can be influenced directly by supervisors.
5. When accidents do occur, they should be investigated promptly for very important reasons, including the fact that information which is gained can be used to prevent accidents in the future.

H. Equal Employment Opportunity
1. The supervisor should endeavor to treat all employees fairly, without regard to religion, race, sex, or national origin.
2. Groups tend to reflect the attitude of the leader. Prejudice can be detected even in very subtle form. Supervisors must strive to create a feeling of mutual respect and confidence in every employee.
3. Complete utilization of all human resources is a national goal. Equitable consideration should be accorded women in the work force, minority-group members, the physically and mentally handicapped, and the older employee. The important question is: "Who can do the job?"
4. Training opportunities, recognition for performance, overtime assignments, promotional opportunities, and all other personnel actions are to be handled on an equitable basis.

I. Improving Communications
1. Communications is achieving understanding between the sender and the receiver of a message. It also means sharing information—the creation of understanding.
2. Communication is basic to all human activity. Words are means of conveying meanings; however, real meanings are in people.
3. There are very practical differences in the effectiveness of one-way, impersonal, and two-way communications. Words spoken face-to-face are better understood. Telephone conversations are effective, but lack the rapport of person-to-person exchanges. The whole person communicates.
4. Cooperation and communication in an organization go hand in hand. When there is a mutual respect between people, spelling out rules and procedures for communicating is unnecessary.
5. There are several barriers to effective communications. These include failure to listen with respect and understanding, lack of skill in feedback, and misinterpreting the meanings of words used by the speaker. It is also common

practice to listen to what we want to hear, and tune out things we do not want to hear.
6. Communication is management's chief problem. The supervisor should accept the challenge to communicate more effectively and to improve interagency and intra-agency communications.
7. The supervisor may often plan for and conduct meetings. The planning phase is critical and may determine the success or the failure of a meeting.
8. Speaking before groups usually requires extra effort. Stage fright may never disappear completely, but it can be controlled.

J. Self-Development
1. Every employee is responsible for his own self-development.
2. Toastmaster and toastmistress clubs offer opportunities to improve skills in oral communications.
3. Planning for one's own self-development is of vital importance. Supervisors know their own strengths and limitations better than anyone else.
4. Many opportunities are open to aid the supervisor in his developmental efforts, including job assignments; training opportunities, both governmental and non-governmental—to include universities and professional conferences and seminars.
5. Programmed instruction offers a means of studying at one's own rate.
6. Where difficulties may arise from a supervisor's being away from his work for training, he may participate in televised home study or correspondence courses to meet his self-development needs.

K. Teaching and Training
1. The Teaching Process
Teaching is encouraging and guiding the learning activities of students toward established goals. In most cases this process consists of five steps: preparation, presentation, summarization, evaluation, and application.

   a. Preparation
   Preparation is two-fold in nature; that of the supervisor and the employee. Preparation by the supervisor is absolutely essential to success. He must know what, when, where, how, and whom he will teach. Some of the factors that should be considered are:
   1) The objectives
   2) The materials needed
   3) The methods to be used
   4) Employee participation
   5) Employee interest
   6) Training aids
   7) Evaluation
   8) Summarization

   Employee preparation consists in preparing the employee to receive the material. Probably the most important single factor in the preparation of the employee is arousing and maintaining his interest. He must know the objectives of the training, why he is there, how the material can be used, and its importance to him.

b. Presentation
In presentation, have a carefully designed plan and follow it. The plan should be accurate and complete, yet flexible enough to meet situations as they arise. The method of presentation will be determined by the particular situation and objectives.

c. Summary
A summary should be made at the end of every training unit and program. In addition, there may be internal summaries depending on the nature of the material being taught. The important thing is that the trainee must always be able to understand how each part of the new material relates to the whole.

d. Application
The supervisor must arrange work so the employee will be given a chance to apply new knowledge or skills while the material is still clear in his mind and interest is high. The trainee does not really know whether he has learned the material until he has been given a chance to apply it. If the material is not applied, it loses most of its value.

e. Evaluation
The purpose of all training is to promote learning. To determine whether the training has been a success or failure, the supervisor must evaluate this learning.
In the broadest sense, evaluation includes all the devices, methods, skills, and techniques used by the supervisor to keep himself and the employees informed as to their progress toward the objectives they are pursuing. The extent to which the employee has mastered the knowledge, skills, and abilities, or changed his attitudes, as determined by the program objectives, is the extent to which instruction has succeeded or failed.
Evaluation should not be confined to the end of the lesson, day, or program but should be used continuously. We shall note later the way this relates to the rest of the teaching process.

2. Teaching Methods
A teaching method is a pattern of identifiable student and instructor activity used in presenting training material.
All supervisors are faced with the problem of deciding which method should be used at a given time.

a. Lecture
The lecture is direct oral presentation of material by the supervisor. The present trend is to place less emphasis on the trainer's activity and more on that of the trainee.

b. Discussion
Teaching by discussion or conference involves using questions and other techniques to arouse interest and focus attention upon certain areas, and by doing so creating a learning situation. This can be one of the most

valuable methods because it gives the employees an opportunity to express their ideas and pool their knowledge.

    c. Demonstration
The demonstration is used to teach how something works or how to do something. It can be used to show a principle or what the results of a series of actions will be. A well-staged demonstration is particularly effective because it shows proper methods of performance in a realistic manner.

    d. Performance
Performance is one of the most fundamental of all learning techniques or teaching methods. The trainee may be able to tell how a specific operation should be performed but he cannot be sure he knows how to perform the operation until he has done so.
As with all methods, there are certain advantages and disadvantages to each method.

    e. Which Method to Use
Moreover, there are other methods and techniques of teaching. It is difficult to use any method without other methods entering into it. In any learning situation, a combination of methods is usually more effective than any one method alone.

Finally, evaluation must be integrated into the other aspects of the teaching-learning process.

It must be used in the motivation of the trainees; it must be used to assist in developing understanding during the training; and it must be related to employee application of the results of training.

This is distinctly the role of the supervisor.

www.ingramcontent.com/pod-product-compliance
Lightning Source LLC
Chambersburg PA
CBHW081810300426
44116CB00014B/2303